BE STILL
AND
put your PJs on

52 RESTFUL DEVOTIONS FOR WOMEN

BroadStreet
PUBLISHING

BroadStreet Publishing Group, LLC.
Savage, Minnesota, USA
Broadstreetpublishing.com

BE STILL AND PUT YOUR PJS ON

978-1-4245-6079-0
978-1-4245-6080-6 (eBook)

Entries composed by Michelle Cox and Sylvia Schroeder.

Design by Chris Garborg | garborgdesign.com
Editorial services by Michelle Winger | literallyprecise.com

Printed in China.

20   21   22   23   24   25   26   7   6   5   4   3   2   1

Introduction

Have you ever been in the middle of a long day and whispered to yourself, "I am so ready to put my pajamas on!" There's something special about PJs. (Especially those cute ones with fancy shoes, cupcakes, or coffee mugs.) Jammies are an indicator that you're home. Add some fuzzy slippers and feel the comfort of being at ease after an exhausting day.

For many of us, rest is something that is almost foreign. It's out of reach on most days. We know better, but we fill our days with enough tasks to keep six people busy. And then we wonder why we're tired, grouchy, or don't feel like doing anything.

It's time for us to use the commonsense God gave us: to realize that rest is a *good* thing, and that God designed our bodies to need it. For most of us, that's going to require some changes. Are you ready?

It's time for a "Come to Jesus" moment. Literally. It's time to come to him for help in learning to say no. For seeking his guidance in what we need to change so our lives are in better balance.

That's what this devotional is all about. Take a few minutes each day and see what God has to say about rest. Discover how all that crazy busyness is affecting you and those around you.

Be still and put your PJs on. It's a good thing.

CHAPTER ONE

On the Calendar

Oh, that I had wings like a dove;
then I would fly away and rest!

PSALM 55:6 NLT

Back in our grandparents' era, life didn't seem as fast-paced as today. They actually used their front porches, visited with neighbors, family, and friends, and went on Sunday afternoon drives to enjoy the scenery. And that was despite not having all the labor-saving devices that we have today which actually don't seem to be helping a lot to give us restful lives.

Our calendars are crammed with commitments. Our desks at work are piled so high with files that they look like mountains on the verge of toppling. We race from one place to another, annoyed that it took more than a minute at the fast food window or that the red light didn't change as quickly as anticipated.

We awaken our children in the morning and spend the

next hour calling out "Hurry! We're going to be late." Or "What's taking you so long? We've got to go!"

Halfway through the day, we're so tired we don't think we'll make it to the end of the day. We long to get home and put on our PJs and slippers. But even those moments are busy and rushed with dinner prep, clean-up, homework, tasks we didn't get done at work, or getting the children ready for bed.

There's no rest for the weary.

That's where we have to get creative and proactive. We have to plan for rest just like we do everything else in our lives, because it won't just happen. On the days that you are home, add a nap to the calendar. The world truly won't come to an end, and you'll awaken refreshed and ready to get back to your work.

Plug fun weekends into your schedule. Your family is a priceless gift from God. They won't remember all the times you mopped the floor, but they will remember the moments you laughed together and made memories.

And the best rest of all? Be intentional about setting time aside to spend with God. That's where real refreshment and strength come from, and those moments will make the remainder of your day so much better.

Dear Father, I'll admit it. I'm tired. I stay tired. And yet I often feel so guilty about taking time to rest. Remind me that putting my PJs on and resting actually makes me a better person: wife, mom, employee, or otherwise. I don't want people to remember me as a cranky woman, and I realize now that I can't take care of others as well when I'm running on empty. Help me to become intentional about resting more, about carving out time to relax, and to spend time with you. Thank you for the rest that I find in you.

Do you feel guilty about taking a nap or resting? Why or why not?

Napping offers several benefits for creating healthy adults, including relaxation, reduced fatigue, increased alertness, improved mood, better performance, increased reaction time, better memory, and fewer accidents and mistakes.

CHAPTER TWO

The Farmer

You have six days each week for your ordinary work,
but on the seventh day you must stop working,
even during the seasons of plowing and harvest.

EXODUS 34:21 NLT

The farmer pulled his dusty cap from his head and wiped away rivulets of sweat. His hand mixed with the moisture left paths of wet dirt and grime like muddy tracks across his forehead. He held his cap's bill in his big hand then plopped it into place again on the top of his head. He jiggled it a bit back and forth until it fit just right like a bottle-cap back on ketchup. The unconscious gesture repeated every day during harvest season when a window of time drove farmers to work themselves half dead for the gathering in of the year's profit. Rest would come after the grain lay safe in big steel bins.

Ah yes, we may not have the same sticky grunge of the farmer in our jobs, but the insistence of those times hits us with the same urgency when projects call, children cry, or looming deadlines arrive. Calendars beg us for space. Time squeezes us for breath.

In the Old Testament law, God provided rest for the farmer, "even during the seasons of plowing and harvest." A day of Sabbath gave release to body and soul.

Seasons of our lives will come and go with demands. Some of them simply must be met. But our busyness necessitates time set aside for rest. A vacation, a schedule-cleared weekend, or even an hour in the day for a short nap are blank slates worthy of planned forethought. This is the stuff grown-up-pajama-rests are made of—we let the tightness of mind and body unravel.

God himself initiated rest. Surely it must be valid for us as well.

The farmer put his tractors in the shed, his tools in their designated spots, and trusted God with the safety of his crops for twenty-four hours while he went to church and then slept away most of the afternoon. For someone whose livelihood depends on a few weeks to gather grain, a Sabbath from work was an act of discipline.

Rejuvenated, the farmer discovered what we all do, the rest was time well spent.

Dear Father, I have such a difficult time stopping to rest. I can't quit until I'm done, but I am never done. Would you help me discipline myself to let go? I want to give you the hours of my day and the to-do lists on my calendar. I recognize my hold on getting things done shows I lack trust in you, that you can help me accomplish the things you want. Help me to believe you really do hold my time and remind me that you've got this when I am trying to do too much. I give you my lists. Thank you, because I know your plans are always best.

Do you practice times of Sabbath rest?
What might need to change to
give space for Sabbath?

Rest is powerful for your body and mind according
to science. A pattern of regular work breaks
reduces inflammation and risk of heart disease.
Scientists also believe it profits the
immune system.

CHAPTER THREE

Gift of Rest

Let us think of ways to motivate one another
to acts of love and good works.

HEBREWS 10:24 NLT

Amusement appeared on faces throughout the
restaurant as the group approached the hostess stand. This
wasn't your normal group of friends out for a fun and
restful night. No, it's not every day you see five dads out for
the evening with their fifteen collective children. Fifteen!
Babies in arms. Toddlers clutching their daddy's hand. And
an assortment of boys and girls ranging from about three to
twelve. Daddy's Day Care had arrived complete with wiggles
and giggles. Can't you just imagine that scene?

But they made it through the evening of controlled
chaos and arrived home with all their children. The main
mishap of the evening came in the form of one little girl
whose dad hadn't noticed she'd had two and a half cups
of apple juice and five kinds of syrup on her pancakes. She
ended up sick in the bathroom and her dad had to get

someone to make sure the ladies room was clear so he could check on her.

Just thinking about what that evening must have been like provides chuckles, but you know what? Those dads were there with all the kids because they had given their wives a weekend to rest. The women had two days with no children pulling on them or calling, "Mommy!" The moms shopped, enjoyed leisurely meals, and sat in the cabin in their pajamas and laughed and talked for hours.

They rested.

Rest is a gift we can give to others who desperately need it. Ask God to show you a single parent, an elderly person, a caregiver, or a weary mom who needs some rest, and then become God's hands and feet to provide those moments for them. Maybe it's buying their dinner so they don't have to cook or staying a few hours with their health-afflicted loved one so they can have a time to themselves. Give someone the gift of rest and discover the blessing during the process. That night when you put your pajamas on and go to bed, you'll also know you've pleased the heart of God.

Father, there are people all around me who are facing difficult circumstances. They're exhausted physically and emotionally. Thank you for your precious promises that you will give us rest. Give me eyes that see the cares of others and give me a tender heart so I may help to ease their load and give them rest along the way. Show me ways I can help refresh them. Give them nights when they can put their PJs on and truly rest. Thank you for the blessing of being part of your plan. And thank you for all the times that you and others have encouraged me when I was going through difficult times.

Think of two people who need rest.
What are some specific steps you can
take to help them?

Sleep is much more than just a passive experience
for your body. Although we might be resting, our
body is engaged in another type of activity, a
process that will bring restoration and healing to
frazzled organs, nerves, and body tissues.

CHAPTER FOUR

Stormy Weather

Suddenly a furious storm came up on the lake
so that the waves swept over the boat.
But Jesus was sleeping.

MATTHEW 8:24 NIV

Have you ever been in a deep sleep and then been jolted awake by a boom of thunder or a bright bolt of lightning? It's an instant awakening, and then it's often impossible to get back to sleep. We lie there seemingly for hours, and just as we get back to sleep, another big boom jerks us awake. Might as well get up and make a cup of coffee because the night of rest is over.

Perhaps you've heard a frightened voice calling, "Mommy! I'm scared!" Or maybe you've heard little footsteps running down the hall and then a pajama-clad child jumps into bed with you and a quivering body snuggles close. They know where to run in a storm.

Storms often roll in with the leaves on the trees whipping about and wind gusts howling. Then a drenching rain begins, plastering everything in its path. Those are the storms where lightning and thunder are intense and streams overflow their banks.

You know what? We have storms in our lives as well. Sometimes they roll into our homes with the power of those intense booms of thunder and bolts of lightning. We're hit by howling winds of adversity such as a phone call from the doctor, a financial crisis, a shattered relationship, or a prodigal child. We sure don't like those storms, and often they hang around far longer than we want.

Those are times that it's hard to have a grateful heart, but God wants us to praise him in the storm. In it—not after it's over. In these moments we can pray, "God, I don't understand, but I know I can trust you. Show me what you want me to learn from this experience."

Just as that frightened child clings close during a storm, cling tight to Jesus. Trust him. Our Father will be with us during the storm, and there's no safer place that we can take refuge—even if we're not in our pajamas.

Dear Lord, the storms in my life have caused me many sleepless nights. My tears wet my pillow. My mind whirls with circumstances that I can't fix, and no matter what I try, I can't make the situations better. Teach me to run to you and draw close to you when I'm afraid. Help me to trust you while I'm still in the storm, knowing that you are always faithful. Remind me to place my heartaches in your hands and stand firm in my faith even while the storms of life howl around me. When the storm is over (because storms always end) help me to share with others about my amazing God.

Why do you have so much trouble turning your storm-filled moments over to God? How does that affect you, and how do you feel when you finally place those situations into God's hands?

Gentle rain provides a calming, white noise effect at night, but noisier storms can wake you up or make it harder to fall asleep. Thunderstorms and bad weather can create plenty of anxiety as well.

CHAPTER FIVE

Perfect Pillow

Jesus said to him,
"Foxes have holes, and birds of the air have nests,
but the Son of Man has nowhere to lay his head."
LUKE 9:58 ESV

Try finding just the right pillow and you will soon discover exactly how spoiled we are. Choices fill the aisles of department stores. Pillow varieties include size, shape, firmness, and materials. Price tags run the gamut from reasonable to outrageous. Each advertise the sleep benefits of their product. For many people worldwide, the hunt for the best pillow isn't an issue. Countless are simply grateful for a place to rest their heads.

A place to sleep gives us shelter from the elements, protection, and belonging. It provides security. It brings rest.

Probably all of us know the feeling of trying to stay awake, but no matter how hard we try, our eyes won't stay open. Many of us have experienced the head-jerking effect of falling asleep while sitting up. Whether in a car, plane, or chair, it is both uncomfortable, startling, and even embarrassing. A pillow to lay against allows us to relax and give in to sleep.

In a passage counting the cost of discipleship, Jesus answers an eager follower who believes he is ready to follow the Master anywhere: "The Son of Man has nowhere to lay his head."

Jesus' home was a heavenly one. He recognized his belonging didn't come from a house or his own bed. He wasn't concerned about the feathers or foam in his pillow. He wanted his disciples to have the same mindset. This life of work and toil, full of unrest and hardship, will never be our forever home. We are passing through, and there is something much better ahead.

Jesus travelled, taught, and healed. He worked long hours and faced opposition and many discomforts. Through his life, he prepared his followers for what was coming, and he journeyed steadily toward the cross.

Our struggle here, the tossing and turning, our cry for comfort and belonging, finds its answer in Jesus. He came to make his dwelling in us by providing for us the possibility of a home not made with wood or stone. An eternal home. That is security where we can lay our heads and find true rest.

Dear Father, I am so glad for a place to lay my head tonight. Every bone in my body is ready to sleep. Thank you, Jesus, for coming to provide an eternal home in heaven with you someday. Help me to learn to be a disciple willing to follow you no matter where it takes me. Give me a heart for others who don't have a comfortable place to lay their heads. Show me how I can help meet people's physical needs and point them to you so they might know true rest. As I fall asleep tonight, I am thankful to you for this place to lay my head, safe and secure.

What makes you feel safe and secure at night? What comes to your mind when you think of Jesus without a place to lay his head?

Pillows should support the natural curve of your neck. If a pillow is too high, it can put your neck into a position causing muscle strain on your back, neck, and shoulders.

CHAPTER SIX

The Fancy Mattress

The eternal God is your refuge,
and underneath are the everlasting arms.

DEUTERONOMY 33:27 NIV

Princesses of long-ago fairy tales might find themselves in for quite a surprise if they took a stroll through most furniture stores today. Choices abound. Gels, coils, foam, latex, and hybrid mattresses promise to deliver a good night's sleep. Some guarantee to keep us cool and others snugly warm. While some are soft, a variety are firm. Advertisements assure us mornings without aches, pains, or headaches. But no one can vow a pea won't slip underneath to disturb our sleep—as happened to a fabled princess.

Often the tiniest things keep us up. Something said or heard, an unsolved puzzle piece to a project, or uneasiness about an almost completed task. They are like that proverbial pea under the mattress. Seemingly insignificant but bothersome.

We wonder, *Did I do that right? What did they mean? What if I said the wrong thing?*

We shift weight, turn from one side to another searching for comfort, looking for that lovely elusive drift into our black dreamy hole. With bedframes that raise and lower, bend and flatten, our beds can do almost everything except fix our morning coffee. But one look at a baby in the arms of a mother or father confirms even the best bedframe and mattress can't compete. Nestled in all sorts of uncomfortable positions, with those parental arms supporting underneath, babies sleep through everything.

As someone who travelled a lot, Moses that great leader of God's people, must have slept in all sorts of places and laid on all kinds of makeshift mattresses. Yet, he penned in the book of Deuteronomy a beautiful reminder, "God is your refuge, and underneath are the everlasting arms." What a wonderful thought as we wind down and push away those thorny twinges ready to poke us awake.

When you find yourself pivoting on your bed at night, with one tiny little niggle that won't go away, here is a thought to banish the annoying discomfort. God is the refuge we can lean into. God's arms hold us. He offers himself, our true rest, as our best cushion.

Dear Father, I confess, there are things tonight that are on my mind: tiny bothersome thoughts. I know you are my refuge, and knowing this brings great peace and comfort, but I am still restless. Please help me relax in the mattress of your care. I can trust you with everything, from the littlest to biggest things, but I don't always do that. I love the thought that your arms are under me. Thank you for being my eternal shelter. Forgive me when I forget that your arms are always available. I want to nestle myself in your love tonight.

**What seemingly insignificant things
bother you at night? Why?
How can you change that?**

Mattresses in one form or another have been
around a long time. The word comes from Arabic
and means, "something thrown down." The oldest
known mattresses used natural materials like
straw, feathers, or horsehair as filling.

CHAPTER SEVEN

Home Alone

"Be strong and courageous! Do not be afraid and do not panic
before them. For the Lord your God will personally go ahead of you.
He will neither fail you nor abandon you."

DEUTERONOMY 31:6 NLT

Have you ever stayed alone in a strange house (or even
alone in your own home)? Your imagination works overtime.
Every creak of the floor is someone sneaking through the
house. The tree branch that slaps against the window is
somebody trying to break in. Or even more nerve-wracking
is the moment when you're sound asleep and you're jolted
from your rest by the sound of loud music. You shake from
fear, and then realize that somebody left the clock radio
alarm set to play music for a wake-up call.

Or perhaps you are home alone and cranked back in the
recliner reading a mystery novel. You're all comfy cozy in
your pajamas with a warm blanket tucked around you and
a cup of hot tea beside you, enjoying the peace and quiet—
when all of a sudden, several loud clunks echo through the

house. Spider legs of fear creep up your spine, and then it dawns on you that it was just ice cubes falling from the ice maker.

Oh my, we've all been there, haven't we? And some of us have amazing imaginations when it comes to moments like that.

Or maybe it's not just your imagination. Maybe those scary sounds are real and a man pounds on your door in the middle of the night or your security system alerts you to an intruder while you're home alone.

That's when it's so precious to know that nothing can happen to us unless it comes through God first. The truth of the matter is that we're never alone, and a 911 call to Jesus is always heard immediately and always has a response. There's such a precious security about that.

God knows what the future holds for us and he promises to go ahead of us on the journey. Did you get that? We'll never end up anywhere that he hasn't already been. God promises to be with us and that he will give us rest. We never have to worry about him abandoning us—even when we're home alone in our jammies and our imaginations have run wild.

Father, whenever I'm home alone and scary things go bump in the night, I'm so grateful to know that you are always with me. Thank you that I can call out to you and know that you're never too busy to listen or to respond. Teach me to trust in you in a fresh new way. Remind me to call on you as my first response, not my last resort. Thank you for always being with me and for your promise that you will never abandon me. You've never failed me yet and I know that you will never fail me in the future. I'm so grateful for the peace of that.

How does it change things to know that you're never alone? What difference does it make to know that God goes before you in every circumstance?

Anxiety consumes the attention of both brain and body. When our stress response system is activated, almost all the other processes in the body and mind shut down.

CHAPTER EIGHT

Better than Sleep

My mouth will praise you with joyful lips,
when I remember you upon my bed,
and meditate on you in the watches of the night.

PSALM 63:5-6 ESV

What can possibly feel better after a day of hard work than the invitation of a soft bed? What could be more inviting than sinking a weary head into the pillow? Or offer sweet soul satisfaction like a quiet house asleep? Unless of course it's neither asleep nor quiet.

For all the bumps in the night, from snoring nearby, to the dog barking next door, to the baby with a fever, or bad pizza, we have our reasons for tossing and turning. All of them are frustrating.

When sleep doesn't come, some people pick up a book. Others warm a glass of milk. When tricks don't work— because nights without sleep happen—what should we do?

The Psalmist must have had sleepless nights too. David wrote Psalm 63 in the wilderness. He undoubtedly had plenty of reasons for insomnia. A makeshift bed, enemies out to kill him, and wild animals roaming about to name just a few. But he also found something better, a higher purpose even more satisfying than sleep in the wilderness.

His nighttime satisfaction came from remembering God while he lay on his bed. He praised God in the watches of the night, and through those long, lonely hours. Intentional praise during nights when sleep doesn't come is a wonderful way to remove cares and tension. We turn our thoughts from ourselves and point them in the direction of gratefulness.

What things can we praise God for when all we want is shut-eye? Start with his character and attributes. Thank him for his holiness, greatness, and goodness. Praise him for your blessings: the house, bed, your family, and job. Thank him for unexpected time with him in the middle of the night, for his Word, and for his will.

As you lay in your bed praising God, you discover how much you have to praise God for, and as the list grows, so does contentment. His blessings are everywhere.

A grateful heart finds the kind of joy and satisfaction the Psalmist speaks about. You may even decide insomnia can be a blessing in disguise.

Dear Father, you give me so many blessings, and I want to thank you tonight for many of them. Thank you for daily necessities and providing for my needs. I praise you for your holiness and mercy. You give joy and satisfaction unlike anything or anyone else. Tonight, even though I am tired, I'm awake. I want to praise you right here on my bed in the dark. I want to meditate on you and remember what great things you have done. I know you see me and understand my need for sleep, but I am grateful for these quiet moments when I can worship you.

**How does praising God bring you joy?
How do you think it affects his heart
when you praise him?**

University research has shown that gratitude is associated with dozing off faster and sleeping longer and better.

CHAPTER NINE

Rest for the Weary

Those who hope in the LORD will renew their strength.
They will soar on wings like eagles;
they will run and not grow weary,
they will walk and not be faint.

ISAIAH 40:31 NIV

Have you ever been totally exhausted and all you wanted was to go to bed and rest? Perhaps you were returning home from a trip with a long flight complete with multiple delays. The constant activity and packed days of your trip combined with a major case of jet lag left you so tired that you collapsed onto the bed without changing out of your clothes or putting your pajamas on. And without even climbing under the covers. Sound familiar?

For some, overwhelming tiredness is from long days at work with overtime thrown in. If we don't finish our paperwork before we leave the office, we have to take it home and work on it so that we'll be ready the next morning. But after months of this unrelenting schedule, we can become so weary that when we go to bed at night, we can't get to sleep for hours because our minds kept whirling with all the details of the day. When we finally fall asleep, it feels like we only sleep for minutes before it's time to get up again.

The good news is that God promises to give us rest and renew our strength. But we also have some responsibility to learn to say no when faced with decisions. We don't have to work all the overtime. That is often a choice, but it was affects our health, and since we are so exhausted that we don't feel like doing anything else, it also impacts those around us—and even our church attendance or time with God.

Wow, it's hard learning to say no, isn't it? Balance is necessary. That's where it's helpful to ask God to be the keeper of our calendars. To pray about our choices before we say yes to adding new tasks to our already busy days. If we allow him to make those decisions for us, he promises us something beyond amazing: rest for the weary. Put your pajamas on and enjoy the sweet restful sleep that's a true gift and blessing from God.

Dear Lord, I'm the world's worst when it comes to saying yes to every opportunity that's presented to me. Remind me that I truly can't do everything and do it all well. Teach me to ask you first before I commit to new tasks. Show me how to find balance as I make choices. Give me wisdom to know whether opportunities are just good things or whether they're God-ordained things, and help me to put you first, my family second, and then other commitments after that. Thank you for your promise of rest. I don't ever want to take that for granted.

Why is it so hard to say no when opportunities come your way? What are some commitments you've taken on and then realized they weren't what God had planned for you? What did you learn from those moments?

Recent research has shown that women today are less happy than they have been over the past forty years. There are many theories about why, but lack of free time is a major reason.

CHAPTER TEN

Sleep Like a King

That night the king could not sleep;
so he ordered the book of the chronicles,
the record of his reign, to be brought in and read to him.

ESTHER 6:1 NIV

Some nights we collapse into bed. Other nights it's a long, delicious process of winding down and letting the day's busyness melt away. You may have a bedtime routine which helps you relax—a book, a hot bath, or a nice cup of chamomile tea. Atmosphere may be important. A candle and soft music set the stage. Getting prepared for a good night's rest is a personalized affair. Most of us would not choose King Xerxes' strategy in the book of Esther, however the sheer boredom of reading records would likely put any of us to sleep.

If we, like King Xerxes had a logbook with all the things we've done, all the places we've been, the good and bad experiences of our lives, it would likely surprise us to see the packed timeline of our existence.

I did what? Ah, yes, I remember going there. What a super time that was.

We might be amazed by our experiences. "Didn't see that coming," we'd say in hindsight.

Perhaps rather than lull us to sleep, our eyes would open wider. Time frames roll through like film shots of events and happenings. Illness, healing. Job success and career failure. Pain and joy. And then, as happened in the reading of Xerxes' true-life drama, we might remember with a sense of dearness the kindness of someone when it was most needed.

Let your mind wonder as Xerxes' did when he asked, "What has been done for this person who helped me in a situation of my need?"

God uses even sleepless nights for his purposes. Can it be God has your eyes open and mind alert for an unseen reason? Your reason may be as simple as prayer. Perhaps someone needs intercession and you are awake for that purpose. Perhaps someone needs encouragement. Maybe you need to say thank you to a friend.

God used the king's sleepless night to express gratitude for a past blessing. But ultimately his insomnia humiliated God's enemies and saved a nation. His tedium of lists and events proved to be part of a much greater plan.

Dear Father, here I am. Eyes wide open again, looking into a dark room. I would rather be sleeping, but I can't seem to fall asleep. Is there a reason you want me awake? Would you filter the thoughts I'm thinking so only those thoughts you desire come into my mind? I am listening, Father. If I should be praying for anyone, would you bring them to my memory? Is there encouragement someone needs? Have I forgotten to thank someone? Thank you for all the times in the past you have walked with me. I'm so glad I can count on you for tomorrow too.

Do you sometimes waken with someone
on your mind who you think needs prayer?
What do you do?

Studies have shown that reading reduces stress
levels by almost 70%. Apparently it only takes
about six minutes of reading for stress levels
to be reduced.

CHAPTER ELEVEN

Too Excited

Yes, my soul, find rest in God;
my hope comes from him.

PSALM 62:5 NIV

Emma was just too excited to sleep. She squeezed her eyes shut tight and clenched her fists under the covers. Red-glossed fingernails dug into her palms, as if the pure joy inside couldn't be contained. She smiled into the darkness and broke the silence with a "Yessss!" She could hardly wait for tomorrow. But first she needed some sleep, and it wasn't going to come easily.

Has excitement ever kept you awake? Sometimes even enthusiasm robs sleep and makes it difficult to relax. When a big event is approaching and you want to be well rested, it can be really difficult to relax enough to grab those necessary winks. When your brain is wired and muscles taut with elation it's frustrating to roll like a rolling pin kneading the bed. Expectations make true rest a challenge.

The Psalmist David knew where to find his rest. "Yes, my soul, find rest in God," David said.

David affirmed his hope came from God because he believed God. He found rest when he placed his expectation in God rather than in circumstances. When David wrote Psalm 62:5, he wasn't anticipating something wonderful, actually he was facing a dire situation. Yet the Psalm speaks of rest, hope, and peace. God cares about sad and happy times. David could trust God for the rest his soul needed.

We hope for good results from a test, a restful vacation, or a clean house. It brings anticipation and delight for what lies ahead. It helps us enjoy life and look forward to the future. Hope sweetens life.

When a big day is ahead, it's always good to talk to Jesus about it. He shares your joy. Like David, remind yourself your soul rests in God. Remember what David said, "My hope comes from him." He is the only one who deserves your every expectation.

Dear Father, I am wound so tight with excitement. I'm like a coil ready to spring. Tomorrow is such a big day. You know how much I've looked forward to this. Thank you for giving me this opportunity. Thank you for bringing me this joy. I'm so happy, I can't sleep. My soul needs to find its rest in you tonight. Would you help me to be at peace so my body can relax? You are my true hope. I have so many reasons to be glad tonight, but most of all I am thankful I can trust you. You are a good Father and I praise you.

**When was the last time you were so
excited you couldn't sleep? What would
you do next time to find rest?**

Excitement increases our cortisol levels. Commonly
known as the stress hormone, cortisol can increase
blood pressure and heart rate—the exact opposite
of what we want when trying to fall asleep.

CHAPTER TWELVE

Sleep Isn't Enough

Each time he said, "My grace is all you need. My power works best
in weakness." So now I am glad to boast about my weaknesses,
so that the power of Christ can work through me.

2 CORINTHIANS 12:9 NLT

No matter how much Lynn rests or sleeps, it's never
enough. With rosy cheeks and a bright smile, she looks
healthy as can be, but sometimes looks can be deceptive.
Lynn has multiple chronic health issues such as an
autoimmune disorder, fibromyalgia, and other medical
problems that cause overwhelming fatigue and pain. None
of these things are visible to the naked eye, but they're
apparent to her on a daily basis—and she's just one of
millions of folks who deal with similar problems.

Where many people get six or eight hours of sleep and
wake up the next morning refreshed and energetic, Lynn
often wakes up feeling as if she hasn't even been to bed. Her
best description of her life is that almost every day feels as if
she's getting over a month of the flu. Some days she doesn't

even get out of her pajamas because she doesn't have enough energy to do so.

That sort of fatigue and pain can lead to depression and despair, but you'd never know it by meeting Lynn. Her sweet spirit and smile touch everyone she meets. No, her circumstances didn't miraculously get better. She's still fatigued. She still hurts every day. And, no, she doesn't like having a chronic illness. But she's learned that God's grace is enough for the difficult days.

She's discovered that her health issues have drawn her closer to him than she would have been in any other situation. Her testing times have become her testimony, and she's found that God can use her to comfort others who are going through similar circumstances by sharing the story of how he's been faithful to her.

Lynn has learned to rest in God.

And she's learned that even when she doesn't understand why she has to deal with the fatigue and pain each day, she can trust the one who knows what's best for her.

Perhaps you suffer with something similar. The good news is that God's grace is sufficient, and that even when you are weak, his power can work through you.

Father, having a chronic illness wasn't part of my plans. I don't like being constantly exhausted. I don't like the pain I endure each day. Please show me what you want me to learn through my circumstances. Even though I often don't understand, I know I can trust you and that I can count on you to be with me every step of the way. Show me your power through my weakness and show me your glory as I rest in you.

How can dealing with a chronic illness bring you closer to God? How can you rest in him through difficult days?

Six in ten adults in the US have a chronic disease and four in ten adults have two or more. Chronic diseases are defined broadly as conditions that last one year or more and require ongoing medical attention or limit activities of daily living or both.

CHAPTER THIRTEEN

Throw Troubles Away

Casting all your anxieties on him,
because he cares for you.

1 PETER 5:7 ESV

It might be at the office, or it could be in your house. Perhaps sitting in church or in the doctor's office. It feels either too cold or too hot. If you are married, likely one kicks blankets off while the other pulls them on. The grocery store is like ice when it's hot outdoors, while your workplace is like a furnace in winter. Regardless of the season, it's as if your own personal thermostat is at odds with everyone else's.

You know that feeling of not quite being toasty enough to slip into a deep sleep? Chill seeps into your being keeping you hovered at lukewarm, and before you know it, cold reaches into your bones. You curl as tight as possible willing your own heat to warm your body, but it's just not quite enough. The solution is simple: throw on another blanket.

Or in the middle of the night, sweat breaks out. While blankets add a cozy layer of warmth, too many become uncomfortable. The process kicks in reverse. The solution is simple: throw the blankets off.

Piles of burdens like too many blankets suffocate us. Anxieties feel heavy, cares birth more cares. Concerns chill our bones. Worry brings fear and insecurity.

Peter advises us to throw it off like casting a blanket on a donkey. Fling it away from yourself; let it leave your hands and get rid of it once and for all. Unlike the crazy cycle of nighttime's blanket yo-yo, Jesus offers good riddance from your blanket of cares.

Sometimes we neglect to remember why we needn't keep those worries wrapped around us, and we don't throw far enough. But the reason we can throw troubles away is also in 1 Peter 5:7. God cares for us. What an amazing truth. Not only does he care about what struggles weigh us down, he wants to bear them for us.

Tonight, as you snuggle into your bed, take time to throw all your anxieties and heavy worries onto Jesus. Because he cares for you. Let those words wrap around your heart and soul like a tender blanket.

Dear Father, I am weighed down tonight under a blanket of anxiety. Worries have followed me all day, but I don't want to take them to bed with me. I am so thankful for your care. It amazes me to think you care about what I do, and you want me to throw all that burdens me onto you. Help me to submit each one into your tender care and help me not to pull them over me again. I want to leave them with you, but I know I will need your strength to not pick them up again. I cast all my anxieties on you.

In what ways does anxiety weigh on you? What steps can you take to give those anxieties to Jesus?

The external temperature in your environment affects sleep quality. Too much heat can lead to difficulty sleeping. Turning your thermostat down creates a better environment for good rest.

CHAPTER FOURTEEN

Worse than Oscar

It is useless for you to work so hard
from early morning until late at night,
anxiously working for food to eat;
for God gives rest to his loved ones.

PSALM 127:2 NLT

Marissa was normally a sweet mama. But today she
made Oscar the Grouch seem kindhearted and jovial. When
her son spilled his milk, she usually said "It's okay. Accidents
happen." But on this morning, she snapped at him, fussing
the whole time she cleaned up the milk. She'd already
scolded the kids because their rooms were a mess, muttering
"Do I have to do everything myself?" as she headed down
the hallway.

Later that morning, her children ran into the living room,
shouting, "Mama! Look at this!"

As she grabbed another shirt to fold from the mountain
of laundry on the couch, she grumped, "Do you always have

to be so loud?" She could see hurt replace the excitement on their faces.

With a subdued look, her daughter handed her two pieces of paper and said, "These are for you." And then the children ran from the room.

Guilt overwhelmed her as she opened the papers to discover carefully colored pictures. One of them included the words, "I luv u" scrawled by her son who was just learning to write. The second page included a note from her nine-year-old daughter. "Mommy, we're sorry you're tired. Bobby didn't mean to spill his milk and make a mess. We've cleaned our rooms and Bobby picked some flowers and put them in a glass in the kitchen so you'd know he was sorry. We love you."

Marissa had made a mistake that many of us make—she'd forgotten to take care of herself, and she'd also neglected her time with the Lord. Just as we can't pour water out of an empty pitcher, we can't pour into the lives of others until we're filled up ourselves. With rest. With occasional breaks for fun and relaxation. And by spending time with God.

Do you need to put your pajamas back on? Do you need to hang out with Jesus for a while? Sometimes we forget that God promises to give us rest. And when you're rested and filled with his love, Mama the Grouch will become a much less frequent visitor at your house.

Father, in the midst of my busy days, I rush from task to task, trying to care for everyone around me and accomplish all the things that must be done. And I'll admit it, I'm exhausted. I want to be a woman whose life reflects the sweetness of Jesus. But I'm tired. Give me balance in my life. Help me to care for myself so I can care for others. Remind me that true rest is found in Jesus. Fill me up with you so I will overflow with your sweetness into the lives of those I love.

Do you forget that you need to take care
of yourself so you can effectively care for
others? What are some steps you can take
for the physical and soul care
that you need?

Most of us underestimate how important sleep is.
When we don't get enough sleep, we are prone to
make more mistakes or forget important steps in
processes. This makes us less efficient and more
easily frustrated.

CHAPTER FIFTEEN

Surrounded

Just as the mountains surround Jerusalem,
so the Lord's wrap-around presence surrounds his people,
protecting them now and forever.

PSALM 125:2 TPT

Mountains of duvet's luxuriousness invited from a king-sized bed. Outside, snowflakes like giant feathers drifted down from a gray sky. At the window, the Swiss Alps' faint outline blended sky and earth. In the middle of such an opulent display of God's beauty, rest seemed impossible to resist. A book and bed beckoned with whispers in the wind tapping at the window.

Lovely pictures of dreamy relaxation find easy response from our weary minds and souls. Stress melts. In reality, those perfect pictures do not often materialize. It isn't every day we can halt our busy lives and take a dive into soft clouds of fluffy comforters.

"When I meet this deadline," we say.

Feelings and emotions equate with serene images of

lovely beaches or majestic mountains fed by our tiredness and need. But moments of rest often don't meet our expectations. They are like the dessert that never comes, or a big fluffy bed we don't have time to get into.

"I'll rest after everyone is healthy again," we sigh.

We feel surrounded. Family, job, and responsibilities find their weary cycle into our souls.

"When the holidays are over."

Recharge time is interrupted. True refreshment of body and mind, even when planned, becomes a rare jewel in the continuum of craziness.

"When life settles down a bit."

Perhaps that's why so often in Scripture God himself paints pictures from the nature he created which speaks calm to our souls. While life's demands seem to surround us, he does too. His presence does not wait for us to put our pajamas on or our feet up.

In the rush of life, God reminds us his protection surrounds us. His presence doesn't need to wait for a break or vacation. It is always with us like a solid range of mountains surrounding Jerusalem, unmovable and constant. He offers it daily. It wraps around us, warm blankets chasing away cares, reminding us he is always watching over us. He invites each of us to take a moment to dive into his luxurious rest.

Dear Father, how I feel the need for rest! I am tired and vacation is a long way off. Knowing you are protecting me today and always is a wonderful thought, but I forget it when life surrounds me with its busyness. I get so tired. Help me remember you surround me with your protection. I want to be more conscious of you in all I do. I know you are the best place for me to find rest. Thank you for surrounding me like a mountain range with your presence. Help me to remember that your presence wraps around me always.

How does the idea of God's wrap-around presence now and forever change how you look at rest? Why are you sometimes forgetful about that?

A good night's sleep may help solve difficult problems. Problem solving is linked to REM (rapid eye movement) sleep during which the brain may be more responsive to flexible cognitive processes, allowing you to solve problems that you may not be able to during waking hours.

CHAPTER SIXTEEN

Raging Blizzard

There is a special rest still waiting for the people of God.
For all who have entered into God's rest have rested
from their labors, just as God did after creating the world.

HEBREWS 4:9-10 NLT

Have you ever experienced a blizzard? Snow comes
down so fast that you can't see through the thick blanket
of white flakes. The wind howls about, blowing snow in
every direction. As the intensity of the storm continues,
fluffy whiteness begins to pile up, first in inches and then in
feet, until everyone is stuck where they are as the blizzard
seemingly rages out of control.

Have you ever thought about the fact that our lives are
similar to those blizzards? Responsibilities come into our
days much like those snowflakes. Some days it's like the
beginning of a snowstorm with a gentle stream of tasks. We
can keep up with them and mark the completed tasks off
our lists.

On other days, it's like a blizzard of responsibilities that pile up. Mountains of laundry. Sticky floors. Meals to prepare. Dirty dishes that multiply in the sink and overflow the countertops. Keeping up with assignments is daunting, as is keeping your boss happy, especially when there's work to take home because you didn't finish all of it while you were at the office. Add in a family emergency, and life is suddenly out of control.

Self-care and rest? That seems like the impossible dream. Yes, those howling winds of "I can't keep up with all of this" blow across our days like a blizzard of epic proportions.

Just as God is in control of the blizzards, he's in control of our lives. He sees our weary days. He cares when we feel overwhelmed. He's given us a sweet promise where he says he has rest for us. Spending time in his Word and turning on some calming praise music can take us from feeling stuck in a blizzard of craziness to a blizzard of sweet joy.

Father, most days it feels as if my life is out of control. I hate the feeling that my circumstances are controlling me instead of me controlling them. Things are so far out of whack that I don't even know where to start to get more balance in my life. Remind me that I truly can't do everything and do it all well. Show me what tasks you want me to do for you. Help me to learn to ask you before I accept new responsibilities. Give me clear vision to see what changes I need to make and remind me what is truly important. I'm so grateful you're in control especially when I'm not.

Why is balance important for you? How does taking on too many responsibilities affect you and those around you?

What we know about neurobiology is that a tired body can't access the prefrontal cortex as readily. The prefrontal cortex is the part of our brain with the capacity to envision, to make excellent decisions, and to discern right actions that align with our highest good. Rest helps us keep this part of our brain online and active in our day-to-day lives.

CHAPTER SEVENTEEN

Wide Awake

The one who watches over you will not slumber.

PSALM 121:3 NLT

Lights dimmed the hospital corridors. Machines whirred, stopping and starting. Now and then, the beep of an alarm sounded. Nurses wearing pajama-looking scrubs hurried in and out of patients' rooms without a sound. A mother sat next to a metal-framed hospital bed, her head bent, shoulders heaved as gulping sobs wrenched from her soul. She held her daughter's hand, now covered with tape and tubes.

She'd never been so tired in all her life. Not even when she'd carried her daughter as a baby through nights of colic and fever. There had been sleepless holes of worry during adolescence. And when her daughter left for college, tears burned the pillow in the dark of night. She'd even walked the house with her new granddaughter in the wee hours of the night to give her own mommy-daughter rest. But now, after months of bedside grief, she didn't want to sleep. Even though every fiber asked for it. For if she slept, perhaps in the morning her daughter might be gone.

There are times in our lives when we desperately need sleep but dread it. Our hearts fear what dawn might bring, and our minds cannot imagine the heart's upheaval a sunrise might present. So, we force our eyelids awake, knowing beyond our night there might be life in another form. We fear what tomorrow's morning might bring. We agonize that we may need to learn to live again in a different way with sorrow's companionship.

How wonderful these words in Psalm 121:3, "The one who watches over you will not slumber."

God does not close his eyes and doze. He is not unaware of our plight. He watches over what we can't.

Morning light filtered in. The mom woke with a start and jerked her head from where it cradled near her daughter's shoulder. Her neck and back protested, but none of it registered. She held her own breath until she saw the weak rise and fall of her daughter's chest. In dawn's light she kissed her daughter's forehead and smiled. God had been wide awake.

Dear Father, I am afraid of what tomorrow might bring. I feel weak and so worn. I can't sleep because I don't want another day to come. I am waiting on you. I can't do this alone. My body is weak, my emotions confused, and my spirit faint. Please give me strength to face what is ahead. I need you more than I can say. Thank you for never sleeping. Thank you for always being present in each and every circumstance. My thoughts are in a fog, but yours aren't. I can count on you. Help me do that. Help me sleep knowing you will be wide awake.

Are there times when you are fearful of the dawn? What brings sleep and peace to you in those times?

The fear of sleep is called somnophobia. For those who have it, the idea of falling asleep is terrifying. Some people who have frequent nightmares or sleep paralysis dread the thought of going to sleep at night.

CHAPTER EIGHTEEN

Even God Rested

On the seventh day God finished his work that he had done, and he
rested on the seventh day from all his work that he had done. So
God blessed the seventh day and made it holy, because on it God
rested from all his work that he had done in creation.

GENESIS 2:2-3 ESV

We're the world's worst to say we don't have time to rest.
We have things to do. Worlds to conquer. Responsibilities
that must be done. And then, if—IF—we have a chance
after getting off the merry-go-rounds of our days, we'll
make time to rest. Seriously, when's the last time you truly
rested? When you felt refreshed and ready to tackle your
day? Well, those times of rest don't happen without some
intentional efforts from us. And the first step is giving rest
the important honor that it's due.

Pay attention here, because these next words are
important: Even God rested. If we want to be like him, aren't
we supposed to follow what he does? Rest can have many
benefits, from giving us better health, to improving our

memory and disposition, lowering our stress levels, and even making a difference in how we function each day.

The first biblical reference to rest happened after God finished his creation of the world. Maybe he spent his day of rest on the beach listening to the waves splash onto the shoreline, or perhaps he enjoyed some time gazing at the mountains while tender blades of grass tickled his feet and he inhaled the aroma of the abundant flowers he'd just made. I love the mental image of God resting, enjoying the stunning beauty of his creation.

Here's a suggestion for all of us—let's take time to truly appreciate what God has designed for us. Hanging out with him in his creation is restful and it's a wonderful opportunity to spend time with him and those we love.

There's no way to listen to the splash of a waterfall without feeling the stress ease from your shoulders. It's impossible to look at the vastness of the Grand Canyon or the beauty of the mountains without feeling God's presence giving rest to your soul. God even blessed the seventh day and called it holy because he rested.

God rested. And we should as well.

Lord, you must get so frustrated with me at times. I know what to do, but I sure don't do it a lot. I realize my body needs rest, but I put everything else first, and somehow, those moments of rest don't happen. Help me to remember that even you rested. Remind me to make rest a priority in my life so I can serve you better and be the woman you desire me to be. Your creation beckons. Help me to make time to enjoy the work of your hands, to spend time with my family and friends making memories, and most of all, to spend time with you.

**How does it make you feel
to realize that even God rested?
Why should you follow his example?**

Getting a doctor-recommended dose of sunlight
can also help you feel refreshed and relaxed
by helping regulate your body's melatonin
production. Melatonin is a hormone that controls
your body's internal clock (basically, it makes you
sleepy). The melatonin-producing part of your
brain (the pineal gland) is directly affected by
access to light. The right amount of melatonin
ensures you have a good night's sleep—
and wake feeling rejuvenated.

CHAPTER NINETEEN

A Quiet Place

Because so many people were coming and going that they did not even have a chance to eat, he said to them, "Come with me by yourselves to a quiet place and get some rest."

MARK 6:31 NIV

The sound of hammers pounding nails into pieces of siding, saws screeching as wood was cut, and construction workers yelling for tools or measurements had awakened Nancy for several months—ever since the crew had started construction on the new house next door. The summer months were hot and humid with temps running up to 105, so she could understand why they started so early every morning, but it sure was wreaking havoc on her moments to sleep.

That is, until this morning. When she woke up to utter quietness from next door, she knew something was different. For one thing, she'd slept until her body said it was time to wake up. She felt refreshed and ready for her day. The holiday for the work crew was a holiday for her as well.

Have you ever tried to rest in a noisy place or with people constantly running in and out of the room? Jesus and his disciples were in one of those busy environments. There was such a constant stream of people coming and going that they couldn't eat, much less rest.

That's when Jesus had an idea. He told them to come with him to a quiet place so they could get some rest. There's something about a quiet place that provides healing—physically, emotionally, and spiritually.

When's the last time you had time where you could be still? Where you could rest? Where you could spend uninterrupted time with God? It takes effort to make those moments happen, but oh my, the benefits are priceless.

Time with Jesus provides a rest we can't get any other way. The Bible says that our mouths say what's in our hearts. When our hearts are full of turmoil, stress, and anxiety, unkind words will erupt. We'll hurl impatient words at those we love. But when our hearts are full from quiet times with Jesus, his sweetness will overflow in all that we do.

Jesus has an invitation for you today, "Come to a quiet place with me and get some rest." Will you do it?

Lord, I'll confess—I often let the noise of the world drown out your voice. You beckon and say, "I want to spend time with you," but I let my responsibilities take precedence. Help me to make the effort to carve out some time to spend with you. Help me to turn my mind off to all the voices of the world around me and to listen to your sweet whispers to my soul. Fill me with peace instead of turmoil. Fill me with wisdom instead of me messing up my relationships. Show me how precious it is to spend time with the one who loves me most.

When is the last time you spent some quiet moments with God? How does it affect you when you do, and how can you make that happen more often?

Rest rejuvenates the body and the soul. We are revived when we make time for silence and solitude, time to hear the Lord speaking to us. Perhaps we saunter in the park on a crisp autumn day or listen to a bird's morning song. Resting is balm for the soul.

CHAPTER TWENTY

In Charge

"I am not even worthy to come and meet you. Just say the word
from where you are, and my servant will be healed."

LUKE 7:7 NLT

Most of us like to think we're in control of situations. We
often think we are more relaxed when we're in control. But
no matter how good it feels to be in charge, there are times
when we are relieved to give it up. We realize how much we
can't control. Nothing brings that into reality as forcefully as
sickness—ours—or someone we love.

Luke 7 takes us into a world of one with authority. A
Roman centurion was a military commander who trained
others, ordered assignments, and assured discipline. He had
authority over a hundred men. Trained by his own superiors,
a centurion knew obedience to his superiors and demanded
it from those in his ranks. His soldiers obeyed his command.
They did what he said.

When the officer's servant became ill, the centurion

realized he had no authority over sickness. He wanted to take it away but couldn't. He didn't have authority to do so.

"Just say the word from where you are, and my servant will be healed."

In the same way the centurion gave orders and was obeyed, he believed Jesus' authority could cure his servant's illness. He understood the power of Jesus' command.

We often spin our wheels trying to make things turn out the way we think they should. If you have been labeled a control freak, you know how hard it is to let go. Relinquishing control can be gut-wrenching. But it can also be a huge relief and a giant leap toward rest.

The centurion's friends returned to the officer's house where they found the servant healed.

Jesus praised the Roman's faith. He told the crowd he hadn't seen such faith even among his own people.

Authority is an amazing thing. When we try to manage life on our own, it becomes a heavy burden. If we find rest illusive and sleep impossible, we need to check who's in control. When we submit to Jesus, it takes the weighty yoke of control from us. We find relief and rest because the one in command is worthy of all authority and he has our best in mind.

Dear Father, I am so worn from trying to be in control of my life and all that happens. I yield all that I've carried. I give up trying to have everything just the way I want it. Forgive me for taking control when you are the one who is the true authority. I know you can handle things much better than I can. Help me to relinquish control. Just say the word, Father, and I know you have the authority to accomplish your will. I am so glad you are the commander and I know I can fully trust you. Thank you for being in charge tonight. I will rest knowing you are in control.

**Are there things you find difficult
to submit to Jesus' authority?
Why or why not?
How does it affect your rest either way?**

Holding on to control and letting go of it at the
same time is impossible.

CHAPTER TWENTY-ONE

Accepting Help

Listen to my instruction and be wise.
Don't ignore it.
PROVERBS 8:33 NLT

Kate had burned the candle at both ends for months. In
the middle. On the top. And underneath. With new contracts
at stake for her business, she'd carried her usual workload
and added countless hours of labor to prepare for her
meetings with potential clients. She'd also volunteered for a
variety of things at church and in the community. They were
all good things, but they weren't all God things that he had
chosen for her to do.

Her body had screamed "I'm tired!" at her for a long
time. The message went unheard and her crazy workload
continued to expand. The messages from her body became
louder, "I need rest. I must have some rest!" She heard it but
ignored what it was saying. Her co-workers were worried
about her and they'd offered to help with various tasks for

the potential client meetings, but Kate had carried on doing everything herself.

Then the day came when her body said, "I've had enough. There's nothing left." Kate had no choice but to listen this time. The all-over weakness and the tremble in her legs left her unable to do anything. The dizziness and weird heartbeat scared her. She'd pushed herself to complete exhaustion and there were consequences to pay.

Over the next few weeks, Kate made some important discoveries: when God nudges our bodies to yell at us, we'd better listen. He's designed us to do the work of one person not multiple people. Kate learned there's nothing wrong with accepting help—or even asking for it. She found the world didn't fall apart when she delegated to her employees. In fact, they added new insights she hadn't thought about.

Most important of all, Kate learned that when she slowed down and listened to her body's nudges, she was caring for the temple that God had given her.

A woman who listens to God's instruction and doesn't ignore it is truly wise. Are you listening when he sends those nudges that you need rest? Don't wait until the bad consequences arrive. Make those changes now. Listen.

Father, you remind me that you will instruct me in the way I should go. To listen to your instruction and be wise and not to ignore it. I so often gloss over those moments when my body says it's tired. I push and push until nothing is left. Help me to remember that I was designed to do the work of one person not two or three. Make me sensitive to your nudges not to accept new responsibilities that aren't part of your plan for me. It seems I'm sometimes slow to learn, so those might need to be hard nudges for your problem child. Teach me to rest.

When was the last time you pushed your body past the limit? How did that affect you physically, spiritually, and emotionally?

If you begin to feel run down, physically or mentally, it might be a sign that you need a break and have reached your limits. In order to keep going and stay strong in life, it's best to have a balance of goals, worries, and urgencies along with fun and restful activities with others and by yourself.

CHAPTER TWENTY-TWO

Paying the Bills

"Your Father already knows what you need before you ask him."

MATTHEW 6:8 TPT

Has worry about finances ever kept you awake? Not only can making ends meet keep us awake at night, the worry makes us miserable. How will we pay the bills? What if we can't make the house payment? How will we live? Financial stress can cause extreme anxiety—as a couple in Ecuador learned.

In the kitchen a missionary husband and wife talked. "I don't know what we are going to do," the missionary whispered to his wife. "What are we going to eat?" Cupboards sat empty. An old kerosene refrigerator bare. A muddy Ecuadorian river flowed outside the cement block house where they lived. Inside the fenced backyard, children played.

Not only was the food gone, their money hadn't come. In the early 1960s, ministry life in the little village lacked many comforts. "Let's pray," his wife said.

God knows our needs even before we ask. He saw the troubled missionaries in Ecuador, and he had a plan. Two Ecuadorian men pulled an old wooden canoe alongside the shore where the missionary family lived.

As they neared, the missionary saw two live chickens hanging upside down, their yellow claws captured in the man's grip. A big felt hat shadowed the stranger's eyes. He thrust the brown feathered birds in the direction of the missionary. "For you," the man insisted loudly.

"I can't pay. I have no money," the missionary said, palms raised, pleading the visitor to take the chickens away.

"No, God told me to bring these chickens to the missionary," he answered. "They are free for you." The American stopped, unable to believe his ears.

"Here," the Ecuadorian again pushed the chickens at the bewildered missionary. The two strangers walked back to their canoe and paddled away. The missionary didn't see them again. He never knew their names.

God does not always supply our needs in miraculous ways, but he is never surprised by them. He is our provider and wants us to bring our financial worries to him.

We can rest knowing the Father already knows our needs. Even before we ask.

Dear Father, I have bills to pay and I don't know where the money will come from. I am tied up in worry and I'm not sure what to do. I can't rest. I can't sleep. My mind is whirring through scenarios of what to do, how to make ends meet. Your Word tells me you know what I need even before I ask. Thank you for knowing exactly what my needs are. I recognize you are the one who provides. I acknowledge you know better than I do what's needed and how to make the payments ahead. Please guide me. I will trust you for what I need.

What are some of the needs you have right now? Why is it sometimes difficult to trust God to meet those needs?

An online survey of more than 2,500 adults found 56% of Americans lose sleep over at least one money issue, with nearly a third worried about everyday expenses.

CHAPTER TWENTY-THREE

Keeping the Peace

You will keep in perfect peace all who trust in you,
all whose thoughts are fixed on you!

ISAIAH 26:3 NLT

It didn't take the young couple long to discover laying down a newborn without waking him up was an art. They'd bungled it several times, a bit from clumsiness, and some because their baby liked the warmth of his parents' arms. They tiptoed into their semi-dark bedroom where a white bassinet was parked near where they slept, or more accurately used to sleep, once upon a time before night feedings and crying mews bolted them both upright. Those days of peace had been turned upside down with the birth of this baby boy.

The new father held his tiny son, a small dot blanketed against his broad chest, a precious treasure cradled against his heart. He gazed at his little eyes shut against soft cheeks. Husband and wife smiled at one another and then holding their collective breath lowered him onto his bed.

He lay on his back, his little chest rose and shuddered with the new breaths of a newborn. Can anything paint a better picture of peace than a baby sleeping?

Yet, the perfect peace Isaiah describes is much greater. He uses the word for peace twice in the original Hebrew. Peace, peace. Peace perfected. Isaiah is describing a great depth of peace belonging to those who have placed their trust in God.

We relate peace to many different things. Sometimes peace is acquainted with location, emotion, absence of trouble, or physical wellbeing. But in this passage, Isaiah points us to consider peace as where our thoughts dwell. He encourages us within the turmoil of life to find relief from our unrest in the place we set our thoughts.

What we think impacts our moods and choices. Thought life matters. Changing what we think changes behavior. As you wind down at the end of the day if your mind is stormy and disquieted, God has an important message for you. Fix your thoughts on him. Let him capture them.

Anxious thoughts vanish when they are set instead on God the Father. Peace and trust walk hand in hand.

Dear Father, my mind is whirring. My thoughts are jumbled. I am uneasy and can't find calm. You say you will keep us in perfect peace when our thoughts are set on you. I want that kind of peace, but my mind is all over, thinking all kinds of things. Capture all the strands of my thinking and help me fix them on you. Keep me from stray thoughts that make me anxious. I give my thoughts to you tonight. I want to trust you more. Thank you for your promise of perfect peace. Please let my mind be filled with peace tonight.

What comes to your mind when you think of peace? When do you find it most difficult to trust?

When the brain is idle, wider regions are active than when focused on a task.

CHAPTER TWENTY-FOUR

Slap Happy

A cheerful heart is good medicine,
but a crushed spirit dries up the bones.

PROVERBS 17:22 NIV

Catherine was always a lot of fun. She lit up a room when she walked into it, and she had one of those personalities that made everyone around her feel good. Her friends loved to be with her because she could take simple everyday moments and make all of them seem special. And that woman could tell a story that would have you either laughing or crying—but usually laughing until you cried and your stomach hurt.

She was sunshine to all who knew her. But there was a particular moment that all of her friends loved. They didn't come often, but when they did, they were something to behold. You see, when Catherine got really tired, she didn't become grouchy, she became slap happy. Everything became funny to her, from the bug sliding down the car's windshield, to something somebody said, to dropping a piece of candy on the floor.

Catherine would laugh until tears streamed down her face and she couldn't catch her breath. And then just as she'd almost get back under control, something else would make her laugh even harder. Everyone laughed with her. They couldn't help themselves. Her laughter was contagious.

The Bible says that a merry heart is like medicine to us, and if you're having trouble sleeping, a few hours spent laughing with family and friends might be just the medicine that you need to get a good night of sleep.

Maybe you can also help share that cheer and joy with others who need a hefty dose. Visit a shut-in or an elderly couple. It might have been a long time since someone just sat and talked and laughed with them.

Encourage someone who's going through a difficult time. Bring some laughter into their home and help lighten their load. Bring some sunshine into the life of a single mom. Take her out to lunch or help her clean her house. Talk about Jesus, spread his love, and share some much-needed laughter.

Those moments together will provide rest for their hearts and souls—and it will do the same for you.

Lord, I'm so grateful for friends and family who bring laughter and fun into my life. They're a blessing. Help me to bless others with laughter, to brighten their days, and to share the joy of Jesus with them. Father, you say that a merry heart is like a medicine. It's true. I've experienced that so many times when my heart was heavy, when I couldn't sleep because of worry or stress, and then you sent someone or something into my life to make the laughter bubble over. Thank you for the joy that I find in you. Help that to overflow into the lives of others.

Why does laughter help you sleep better? How can a joyful spirit be contagious to others?

Laughter isn't just a quick pick-me-up. It's also good for you over the long term. Laughter can improve your immune system, relieve pain, increase personal satisfaction, and improve your mood.

CHAPTER TWENTY-FIVE

Secure Feeling

If you lie down, you will not be afraid;
when you lie down, your sleep will be sweet.

PROVERBS 3:24 ESV

While cyber criminals make headlines, and videos of hacked nurseries circle media channels, our security feels shaky at times. Precaution occupies what we do and how. We are attentive to those pesky passwords, credit card use, and unknown callers. After a long day, the last thing we want to put on at night with our comfortable pajamas are those accompanying uncomfortable thoughts of dangers lurking in the night.

Sweet sleep, that goal after a day filled with hectic schedules and cramped expectations dissipates with the fast drumbeat of a fearful heart. We've all been there, eyes wide-open staring into a dark room, ears strained for sound, and our breath held. Insecurity pins us like a blanket wrapped too tight until bit by bit we feel ourselves relax again.

Proverbs talks about security resulting from God's

wisdom. As we incorporate the Word of God into our lives, God brings a different kind of security. Not the type we install with alarms or pay big money for, but the kind that underlies our thoughts and actions. God's security assures us as we end our day. He has walked with us during the hours past and will accompany us in the night ahead.

We rush to appointments and activities, balance the books, and fix meals. It is time to unwind by intentionally taking our eyes away from all the running and doing. Then we can begin to relax by being with God where security dwells.

How silly we would be to put all of our trust in a gadget rather than in God. Tonight, when you close your eyes, train your thoughts to dwell on his truths.

Plan ahead to spend your last waking hours intentionally thinking through the blessings of your day. Look forward to thanksgiving as your head hits the pillow. Remember God's faithfulness throughout the day. Look back and recognize he is your confidence in all you do.

Prepare for sweet sleep with confidence in God. Let truth relax your racing heart and taut muscles. When trust anchors to a secure God, frightening insecurities fade.

Father, help me as I lie down to sleep to relax in your security. Please don't let my thoughts take me down roads of fear and insecurity. I thank you for the many ways you walked with me today and the times you protected me. Open my eyes to blessings you provide tomorrow, so I learn to trust you more. Thank you for being a wise Father. Teach me your wisdom through your Word so I can learn how to rest better in the security you provide. I know you are the one who gives sweet sleep and I ask you to guard me safely tonight.

What makes you feel insecure?
What would those insecurities look like
if Jesus transformed them into securities?

Dreams can occur during any stage of sleep but
they are most vivid during the REM (rapid eye
movement) phase. Everyone dreams for a total of
about two hours per night.

CHAPTER TWENTY-SIX

Not Happy

The Holy Spirit produces this kind of fruit in our lives:
love, joy, peace, patience, kindness, goodness,
faithfulness, gentleness, and self-control.

GALATIANS 5:22–23 NLT

Have you ever gotten out of bed and before your feet hit the floor, you knew it wasn't going to be a good day? You glared at the sunshine streaming in the window. You slammed the clock back onto the nightstand. You stubbed your toe as you hunted for your slippers. And you might have pitched a hissy fit when you discovered the outfit you'd planned to wear to work had a big stain on the front.

The bad attitude continued as you headed to the kitchen. The coffee was too strong (even though that's how you usually like it), and you slammed the refrigerator door when you discovered you were out of your favorite creamer. You moaned when you saw all the bacon was gone, even though you'd been dieting and said you shouldn't have any.

Before you knew it, the people who'd been laughing and

talking before your snarly attitude settled throughout the entire house were now subdued and avoiding whatever room you were in. The final straw was when someone said, "Wow, maybe you need to go back to bed and get up on the other side."

Those bad attitude days don't just occur by chance. Perhaps they're because something happened the day before that hurt us or caused anxiety, wrecking our sleep and making us exhausted the next morning. Maybe we stayed up way too late and didn't get enough sleep. Or sometimes it can even be because we haven't spent enough time with Jesus. We haven't brought our heartaches or anxieties to him. We haven't heard his voice or soaked in his sweetness.

Ultimately, it's our choice as to whether or not we're going to let a lack of rest and a hateful disposition take over our day. What will you choose?

Lord, I don't want to be a grumpy bad-tempered woman, but sometimes I let hurtful words or actions take root in my heart, and then they keep me awake as I dwell on them. Help me to place my heartaches and my burdens into your more-than-capable hands. Then help me to leave them there instead of picking them up again as I so often do. When problems arise, help me to rest in you and your promises. Give me a spirit of sweetness and kindness, and when I make the unwise choice to stay up too late, remind me that a rested woman is a nicer and more loving one.

Why does it make a difference to have God's fruit of the spirit in your heart? Why does it change your ability to sleep when you place your problems and hurts in God's hands?

Sleep and mood are closely connected; poor or inadequate sleep can cause irritability and stress, while healthy sleep can enhance well-being.

CHAPTER TWENTY-SEVEN

Be Still and Know

Be still, and know that I am God!
I will be honored by every nation.
I will be honored throughout the world.

PSALM 46:10 NLT

"Shhhh. Sit still." A few church pews ahead sat a mom and her little girl. Being still was not the girl's forte. Black curls bounced like wired springs around an innocent little face. Energy spilled from every inch. She jiggled herself farther against the bench and looked up for approval. Mom put a warning finger to her lips.

Being still is difficult for many of us. A wiggle in our dissatisfied souls begs for more. There is an incompleteness inside, and it is not only disruptive, it is deceitful. Stillness means different things to different people and ages. Being still to a two-year-old is poles apart from that of a sixty-year-old. Yet, the internal struggle may not be all that dissimilar.

Silence can be uncomfortable. To be motionless might almost drive us crazy. It takes effort and requires discipline.

We fill days with activity. We use arms, legs, and brains almost incessantly. We race as if life is a sprint and ping-pong as if bouncing from thing to thing is how we are meant to live. At the end of the day, we look forward to down time. It's time to head for the PJs and cocoa. We want to stop striving.

Relaxing our grip on must-do items and need-to tasks is like prying candy from a dimpled little hand or like a little girl made to sit quietly while she is fairly exploding.

God asks us to cease our incessant striving, to let it fall, drop it. But the truth is, it's difficult to know how. How does the spinning suddenly stop? What does God mean when he says, "Be still?" Be still has a part two.

"Be still, and know that I am God!"

Knowing God is a powerful component to being still. Fretfulness and restlessness calm as our knowledge of God increases. We are easily deceived thinking effort compensates what is lacking inside us. Knowing God completes us. Stop and learn by knowing. Acknowledge who he is. Be in awe of him. He will accomplish what we cannot.

Relax. Let it fall. Drop it.

Dear Father, I confess sometimes I just can't be still. I work hard and don't really know how to stop. I want to, but I am restless. I desire to know you better. I want to take the time and effort to sit still with you. I don't want to forget to know you are God all throughout my busy days. Remind me, Father, who you are when I am flustered and tired. Remind me of who you are when I am sad and discouraged. Remind me today when I am working and when I am resting. Help me to stop my striving and know you. You are awesome.

Do you have a difficult time being still?
Why or why not?

Some of the most common causes of chronic insomnia are anxiety, stress, and depression. Difficulty sleeping can make them worse, creating a vicious cycle difficult to break.

Chapter Twenty-Eight

Opposites

I praise you, for I am fearfully and wonderfully made.
Wonderful are your works; my soul knows it very well.

Psalm 139:14 esv

Al and his wife, Pam, are as different as daylight and dark. Literally. He's a morning person. He jumps out of bed all cheery and ready for the day. Pam's just the opposite. Some days it takes her at least thirty minutes or longer before she begins to truly wake up.

When nighttime comes, their situation flip-flops. Al snoozes on the couch while they watch a movie, and then he's in bed sound asleep by nine. Pam, though? That's when she starts to come alive. She can get more done in those next three to five hours than she's accomplished all day. After her tasks are finished, Pam loves to stay up and read, enjoying the quietness of the house and a little time by herself.

God wired them differently and it's something they had to learn to work around in the early days of their marriage. But they love each other enough to embrace their differences. Pam allows Al to get his rest the way his body demands—as an early bird—and since she works from home and sets her own hours, he enables his night owl sweetheart to sleep later the next morning.

All of us are different, uniquely made by the God of the universe. The God who knit us together in the womb, who knew us before we were born, who has a plan for our lives, had a purpose in every tiny detail of our lives.

Al has an occupation where it's important that he begins his day early. God knew that would be hard for him if he was a night owl. Pam needs quietness and solitude to accomplish her work and God knew those moments would arrive after her family went to bed each night.

Sometimes we forget how intricately and wonderfully made we are; yet when the days arrive that we can look back at our lives with the beauty of hindsight, it's so marvelously clear that every seemingly insignificant detail of our lives was arranged by the conductor of the universe. Yes, even the rhythm and rhyme of our sleep patterns.

Father, it overwhelms me when I think of how intricately you've designed us—even down to our sleep patterns. Help me to be sensitive to your plan for me. To see how the seemingly insignificant things in my life are part of the giant map you've laid out for me. I see so often that you've gifted me with every minute detail of what I need to accomplish the tasks you want me to do. Thank you for wiring me the way you did and help me to rest so I can become all that you want me to be.

Are you an early bird or a night owl? Why do you think God wired you that way?

What causes sleep patterns? The answer lies in each individual's biological internal clock, or circadian rhythm, as scientists call it. Some people have longer natural cycles than others. If that's the case, they are more likely to be night owls. Shorter natural cycles typically create early risers.

CHAPTER TWENTY-NINE

God Who Sees

She called the name of the LORD who spoke to her,
"You are a God of seeing," for she said,
"Truly here I have seen him who looks after me."

GENESIS 16:13 ESV

Have you ever felt mistreated? Something we've been through evokes a perfect storm of anger, hurt, and betrayal. It stirs inside our stomachs like acid. And in the dead of night, those feelings of unfair treatment keep us wide awake, unable to relax. Sleep is impossible. In an Old Testament story twisted with injustice, comfort comes where we least expect it.

Sarai, wife of the Israelite patriarch Abraham, mistreated their servant. The entire mess started when Sarai took things into her own hands rather than trusting God. God promised them a child, but Sarai figured God needed help with that since she was already too old. As a result of Sarai's actions, her Egyptian slave, Hagar, became pregnant. With the child of her master, Abraham, growing within her, there was plenty of rancor between the two women.

Sarai treated Hagar so cruelly that Hagar ran away into the desert. She felt abandoned. She wept without hope: alone, and uncared for. But God saw her affliction and all that had transpired. He sent an angel to console her. In the depth of her deep despair, Hagar met the God who sees. He brought comfort to her soul.

"You are El Roi, the God of seeing," Hagar said.

When Hagar felt the brunt of Sarai's abuse, she felt forsaken. But that helpless feeling of being wronged must have changed drastically when she recognized God cared about what happened to her. He was completely aware of her situation; the good, bad, and ugly.

When hurt keeps us up at night, and reels of memory repeat offenses in full color, it is next to impossible to find the peace we long for. We might wish to strike back, or long to get away as Hagar did.

God sees what others can't. He knows what no one else does. Our God sees exactly what you have been through. He's got all the details, and he has not abandoned you.

"Truly here I have seen him who looks after me," Hagar said. As she learned, rest is possible because God is looking after you.

Dear Father, I'm so thankful you see me tonight. I feel so alone. I can't stop thinking about what happened. You know how I've been treated. I'm hurt, and I feel betrayed. Thank you for being the God who sees all. You are my comfort because you know the whole story. You see what others don't. Help me to trust you and to not try to take things into my own hands. Help me to respond in the right way to mistreatment, even as you did when you were on earth. Help me to be able to stop thinking about it. Calm my heart and give me rest from the tense replay in my mind. Thank you for being the God who sees.

How might remembering that God sees calm you when you feel you've been mistreated? How does that affect your rest?

High-quality sleep is defined, in part, by being asleep for at least 85% of the time you are in bed. If you're able to zonk out in short order once your head hits the pillow, you are on your way to quality sleep. Experts say that the ability to fall asleep in thirty minutes or less is a good indication that your sleep quality is high.

Chapter Thirty

Whose Fault

"In your anger do not sin":
Do not let the sun go down while you are still angry,
and do not give the devil a foothold.

EPHESIANS 4:26-27 NIV

She laid with her back toward him. He hugged the edge of the bed, as far from her as possible. The argument still sounded in his ears. Hurt pounded in her heart. Both said things they should not have and neither knew how to resolve what had begun as a simple question. Asked in innocence, it spun a discussion of misunderstood challenges and offenses. Now neither could sleep. He would wake up cranky. She would start her day weepy. Foggy tiredness would continue to spiral their emotions downward and further from a solution.

Conflict is a sure way to a lousy night's sleep. Most counselors agree, relationships prosper when we keep short accounts. Festering anger left to stew rarely benefits anyone. It doesn't help with sleep either. No matter how much we need sleep, tension prohibits us from shutting down the active thoughts that quicken our heartbeats and waken our bodies. Many marriages hold to the policy of resolving marital conflict before heading to bed. It might make for a lot of late nights, but there is reward for a heart and mind at peace.

Perhaps the Apostle Paul considered our sleep when he wrote, "Do not let the sun go down while you are still angry," or maybe he meant as a principle that anger should not simmer, rather it ought to be resolved as quickly as possible. Either way, we know by experience, anger is not conducive to a tranquil night's rest.

There is something bigger at stake than a night's sleep. Anger left unchecked unlocks a door for Satan to push his ugly foot into a relationship and into our lives. Paul seems to be saying to take care of your anger before time passes; don't let the day end while it continues to grow. It will create the kind of rift Satan uses to cause us to sin more.

If you find yourself tossing and turning with the blame game, stop and take it to God. Anger grows in the dark. Slam sin's door. Morning light will shine much brighter when you do.

Dear Father, I am wound tight as a coil ready to spring. Tension is pounding in my head. I feel angry and really want to give in to blame. I know where this is going, Father. I will be miserable during the night and wake up even more miserable unless these thoughts stop and the anger boiling inside of me calms. I don't want to give any space for Satan. Please don't let him gain a foothold into my life. Help me see my own faults and how I have been wrong. Forgive me and give me grace to forgive. Calm my mind and heart. Take the anger and transform it into forgiveness.

**What sometimes makes you angry
at bedtime, and how do you react?
How would you like to handle it?**

Physically, anger increases cardiovascular activity,
which makes falling asleep more difficult.

CHAPTER THIRTY-ONE

My Sheep

"I am the good shepherd.
The good shepherd lays down his life for the sheep."

JOHN 10:11 NIV

There is something soothing about the thought of sheep and shepherds, unless of course you are the one tending sheep. Herding, calling, feeding, leading, and gathering can't be all that easy. After all, aren't people a lot like sheep, and isn't life full of shepherding? Wouldn't it be nice at the end of a day to gather all our cares and leave them inside a pen to stay put for the night?

Busy moms know a lot about shepherding. Dads feel the responsibility of leading their families well. Executives carry concerns for their employees. Politicians seek approval from constituents. Ministers search to present God's Word correctly. Students bear the weight of schoolwork and yearn for accomplishment.

Sometimes at the end of the day, it is difficult to leave those responsibilities behind. We feel uneasy about our ability to protect everything entrusted to us. We aren't sure if we are doing all we should.

Am I leading right? Is the church heading in the right direction? Should I have disciplined my child in a different way?

Like scattered sheep, tasks leap through our minds. Shepherding is hard work. Herding our daily strivings into a safe and protected place and depositing them there would be lovely.

Jesus picked up on the theme of sheep and shepherds. Shepherds in the Middle East often slept in the doorway of the sheepfold. In small villages, folds sometimes backed up to stone walls or caves so only one entrance or exit remained. The shepherd's body protected the sheep from wandering out and wolves or thieves from coming in. With the shepherd as the gate, nobody could mess with the sheep.

Jesus offered himself as the only way into the sheepfold. He is the only gate, and that knowledge provides comfort and peace. He gave us his Word to guide us and lead our steps.

When the cares of our lives scatter through our nights like restless leaping sheep, God wants us to remember who blocks the doorway. No one guards and protects like he does. We can rest easy in his sheepfold.

Dear Father, my mind wants to wander tonight. I made decisions today that impact others. I am unsure, uneasy, and doubtful about whether or not I did the right thing. I feel the heaviness of responsibility. You are my good shepherd. I know you lead and guide me. Keep my heart safe from anything that might carry me far from your will. I trust you to keep and protect me and those I love. I give you each weight I carry. I am so glad I can count on you to guard me tonight. Please hold me tight in your arms.

**What does Jesus as a good shepherd mean
to you right now? How can you release
bothersome cares as you go to bed?**

Counting sheep does not help you fall asleep. In
some studies, subjects took slightly longer to fall
asleep when told to count sheep. They suggest
instead trying to picture relaxing images like a
beach with gentle waves.

CHAPTER THIRTY-TWO

A New Creation

If anyone is in Christ, he is a new creation.
The old has passed away; behold, the new has come.

2 CORINTHIANS 5:17 ESV

Sarah's pajamas didn't feature images of playful kittens, stylish shoes, or mugs of hot cocoa with cute sayings. Her mattress wasn't six inches thick with cushy memory foam on top. She didn't kiss her loved ones good-night and then ease into sleep with soft music playing in the background.

Sarah's pajamas were prison-issued, the same color and formless style as all the other prisoners. Her mattress was thin, the cell cheerless, and she was far from loved ones, both in distance and relationship. The background of noise as the lights dimmed included yelling and cursing before the guards quieted everyone.

In her wildest dreams, she would never have imagined herself in this cell, but she'd started hanging out with the wrong friends and made bad choices as she listened to their voices urging her to try some of their drugs. "It will be fun!" they'd said. "You'll be fine."

But she wasn't. As her life had spiraled downwards, she'd been arrested for drug possession and robbery. Every night when she stretched out to sleep, all she could see in the dark was the image of her mother's brokenhearted face. All she could hear was her tears. She hadn't been able to sleep well since her incarceration. It's hard to sleep when guilt and shame are crushing the breath from you.

But then during a service at the prison, she heard the story of God's love. She learned about a God with grace and mercy, one who could make a new creation out of her messed-up life. The speaker said, "It's like when a caterpillar becomes a butterfly. It never goes back to being a caterpillar again. And when God changes your life, you never have to go back to a life of guilt and shame. You become a new creation."

Sarah asked Jesus into her heart that day, and for the first time in a long time, her sleep was sweet. Are you consumed with guilt and shame? Jesus promises to make you a new creation, and he will give you rest.

Father, for so many years, the guilt of my past haunted me, disturbing my rest and peace. I did so much wrong. I hurt you and others. You said you've made me a new creation. That means I'm not the same as I was, that I'm something different and fresh and clean. Thank you for the life-changing message that I no longer have to be overwhelmed with guilt and shame because you paid the price for me. What a precious and priceless gift. I can never repay you for such sacrifice and love. I'm a new creation in you, and because of that, I can place my head on my pillow and rest in sweet peace.

How does becoming a new creation in Christ provide sweet rest? How has God changed you from your past?

Guilt is a very distressing effect of anxiety. Anxiety and guilt have a mutual cause-and-effect relationship that makes the cycle difficult to break. Anxiety and guilt can cause headaches, stomachaches, muscle tension, sleep disturbances, and more.

CHAPTER THIRTY-THREE

Little People

"The Son of Man came to seek and to save the lost."

LUKE 19:10 NIV

She recognized the feeling after her PJ's wrapped her tired body with its pink soft flannel. As if she could peel off the busy day like her discarded clothes. But those longed for pajamas didn't cover the nagging feeling of under-accomplishment, as if she herself ended the day incomplete. She felt little. Unimportant. Insignificant.

When our bodies are tired and our spirits match, it is easy to look at the great big world and feel very small. We try not to pay attention to numbers, but we do. We see how few likes we get on social media or watch promotions fly by to land on others. We wonder why we are spinning our wheels. Why are the big bucks heading in another direction? And sometimes it hits us.

I'm just a little person.

If anyone might have had a little complex it could have been Zacchaeus in Luke 19. After all, he was known for his short stature. Zacchaeus of Sunday-School-song fame was a little man. His job as tax collector didn't endear him to others. Extracting money from the people did not win popularity. Besides, tax collectors usually weren't the most honest bunch.

Zacchaeus wanted to see Jesus. His height made it impossible to see above the heads of the crowd, so he ran ahead and climbed a sycamore tree. From a limb he watched as Jesus came closer. Jesus stopped, looked up at where Zacchaeus sat and said, "Zacchaeus, come down immediately. I must stay at your house today."

Little people have great value to Jesus. Sooner or later all of us look at the world and compare. The scope of our tiny place in a big world shrinks in our minds as insignificant, and we head to bed wondering if all the rush and hard work has any worth or purpose at all.

"The Son of Man came to seek and to save the lost."

Jesus came for all. He is our salvation and significance. Little people with a great God have a divine purpose. Sleep on that tonight.

Dear Father, maybe I'm just tired. Or perhaps discouraged. I feel so little, so insignificant. I compare myself to others and wonder why I try so hard but seem to get nowhere. It doesn't feel worth the effort. I feel like a nobody doing nothing that's valuable. Help me to find my significance in you. You came to seek and save the lost. Thank you for finding me. I want to follow your divine purpose for my life. Teach me how little people fit into your kingdom to do great things for you. As I head to bed tonight, show my heart your great value and worth, and help me to rest in you.

What makes you feel insignificant, and how does that affect your rest? How do God's purposes change those thoughts?

Too tired to sleep? Overtiredness is blamed the world over when young children have difficulty sleeping, but it also happens to adults. Lack of respite for our minds overloads our brains making us restless.

CHAPTER THIRTY-FOUR

Awakened by God

The LORD came and stood there, calling as at the other times,
"Samuel! Samuel!"
Then Samuel said, "Speak, for your servant is listening."

1 SAMUEL 3:10 NIV

The book of 1 Samuel tells the story of a night when Eli, the priest, and Samuel, the boy, were in their beds. Samuel heard a voice calling him and he ran to Eli, thinking it was him. But Eli told Samuel he hadn't called and told him to go back to bed.

The same thing happened a second time. The boy heard the voice calling him, "Samuel," and he ran to Eli again, but Eli hadn't called him and told him to go back to sleep.

When the lad heard the voice calling him again, he went back to Eli thinking he had called. By now Eli realized what was happening. He knew the Lord was calling the boy. He told Samuel that when he heard the voice again, he should reply, "Speak, LORD, for your servant is listening." When Samuel did that, the Lord told him some truths about Israel and Eli, and that a promise God had made would soon be fulfilled.

It's amazing to think about God talking to Samuel in the dark hours of the night. What a beautiful example for us the next time we're awakened in the wee hours. I wonder what would happen if instead of just lying there staring at the ceiling, we'd say, "Lord, if there's anything you want to say to me, go ahead and speak. Your servant is listening."

What a precious gift to hear his sweet whispers in the darkness, to spend one-on-one time with the God who loved us enough to die for us. What precious fellowship to tell him we love him, to give him our hearts, our souls, our lives, for whatever he desires for us.

We're often so busy that we miss the opportunities to spend quiet time with God. Those be-still moments are priceless. The next time you awaken in the middle of the night and can't go back to sleep, issue an invitation to spend some time talking with Jesus.

Oh, and you might want to hush long enough so you can hear what he wants to say.

Father, the story of young Samuel in the temple touches my heart. My soul cry echoes his, "Speak Lord, for your servant is listening." Give me ears that listen intently for your sweet whispers. When you wake me in the night hours, make my heart receptive to your messages for me. Help me to realize how special and priceless those quiet times are in the night hours with you. Yes, I need my sleep, but even more, I need you, Lord. Thank you for wanting to spend time with me, to speak with me, and for the intimacy of nighttime conversations with you.

Why is it always worth interrupting your sleep to spend time with Jesus? How do you feel after those times?

Rest is interconnected with Jesus. Without rest, we cannot maintain a healthy, abundant life. Why? Because, it rejuvenates us and provides us with the energy we need to honor God and to love our family, friends, and those around us. It is important that we clear our minds, relax our spirits, and rest in knowing that Jesus will take care of our worries.

CHAPTER THIRTY-FIVE

Lists and Lists

The Lord said to her, "My dear Martha,
you are worried and upset over all these details!
There is only one thing worth being concerned about.
Mary has discovered it, and it will not be taken away from her."

LUKE 10:41-42 NLT

They were still sitting across the dining room table from her when Karen realized how much she wanted her guests gone. The ham and mashed potatoes sat cooling between the two couples. Conversation flowed. Everything looked picture perfect, but she was increasingly antsy about the disaster in the kitchen. Karen's mind wandered into a world of later. After her guests left, she'd clean up and put on her pajamas. Tension and hurriedness would melt like butter.

Your to-do lists may not have anything to do with seating people at your table, but with your job, school, or other activities. If you are a list maker, whatever compiles your list seems long and consuming. If you love to cross out accomplishments, the satisfaction is undeniable, as is the agony of what remains, or even worse, what gets moved to tomorrow's list.

Martha, the hostess in Luke 10 had far too much on her to-do list. Her sister didn't seem to be pulling her weight. While Mary sat at Jesus' feet, Martha dripped with sweat. Flustered with preparations, she hurried.

"Jesus, don't you care that I'm doing all the work?" she complained.

"My dear Martha, you are worried and upset over all these details!" Jesus chided.

Many of us identify easily with Martha. After all, the meal couldn't cook itself. But Jesus commended Mary because she chose to be with him. To-do lists only matter for a few hours. Spiritual life counts for eternity. It remains after a lovely meal, after the guests leave, and the clean dishes are put away.

Lists keep us up at night, and they wake us with urgency in the morning. Things to do before bed ticked in Karen's thoughts. The conversation shifted to deeper subjects. Uplifted and challenged, the focus of her attention changed to Jesus. She forgot her tiredness.

Like Mary and Martha, we choose what is truly worth our concern. Lists, lists, and more lists will wait for tomorrow, while sweet rest in Jesus comes tonight.

Dear Father, I have lists of things to do. I am overwhelmed with details. My mind is spinning, and my body is so tired. Give me the spirit of Mary and help me to choose what is most important. Thank you for wanting what is best for me, for wanting me to spend time with you. I know it is so good to be in your presence, to listen to you, and sit at your feet. I give my list to you. Quiet my heart and mind so I can rest in you. I trust you to help me do what must be done and to forget the rest. You are worth every minute.

Are you a list maker? How do your lists reflect what is most important to you? Where does Jesus fit on that list?

When your mind races with things to do the next day, taking five minutes to write them out might help you fall asleep faster according to a recent study. You relax by off-loading the list from your mind to paper.

CHAPTER THIRTY-SIX

New in the Morning

The steadfast love of the Lord never ceases;
his mercies never come to an end;
they are new every morning;
great is your faithfulness.

LAMENTATIONS 3:22-23 ESV

She couldn't even look forward to getting into her pajamas. She'd never actually left them. The baby had been up all night with a fever. *Should I take her to the doctor?* The question dogged her rocking and pacing hours. When the eight-month-old finally fell into a deep sleep, the sun already tinged the day pink. "Should I drop into bed or shower and get something done?" she asked herself. Bone weary, the new mom dragged herself into the shower with a sigh and prayed for a nap.

Every new day is a gift, but they don't always feel like it. Some personalities greet mornings with enough cheer to gag a night owl. Some days dawn bright and sunny, while others are filled with heartache and gloom.

God has given dispositions as varied as the people he created. Regardless if you wake hopeful or hopeless, when the unexpected happens, and there is seriously no rest to be found, remember three things from Lamentations 3.

"The steadfast love of the Lord never ceases." Now that's a thought to bring into a new day. While a new mom may ride waves of ups and downs or a job leaves us feeling good and bad, the Lord's love is steadfast. It doesn't waver or stop.

"His mercies never come to an end; they are new every morning." Regardless of the night before, each morning opens with God's mercy, brand new all over again. And it is endless. With this truth before our barely open eyes, even the most reluctant can get out of bed.

"Great is your faithfulness." God is faithful. He can be trusted with the day ahead. His faithfulness is like his love and mercy. It is consistent and it is great. When the alarm wakes you from your beauty rest, try that thought on with your morning routine.

Love, mercy, and faithfulness clothe each morning with hope after a dark night. No matter if you've been walking the baby all hours or agonizing over a decision, each day God provides all you need.

Dear Father, how can I even begin to thank you for your steadfast love? I am so glad you aren't fickle with your love like I am. Thank you that it is constant and never-ending. I am so grateful your mercy will be new in the morning, waiting for me to wake up. Thank you that it never runs out, even during a rough night. Father, your faithfulness is something I can count on today, tonight, and tomorrow. You give me confidence that no matter how this night goes, you will be with me. I know I can trust you with my night and with my morning.

What does it mean to you that God's mercies are new every morning? How could this change the way you think in the morning?

More women tend to be morning people, while more men lean toward being night owls.

CHAPTER THIRTY-SEVEN

Crazy

It is in vain that you rise up early and go late to rest,
eating the bread of anxious toil;
for he gives to his beloved sleep.

PSALM 127:2 ESV

Do you sometimes have moments when you accomplish a tremendous amount, and for just a few minutes you feel like Wonder Woman? Unfortunately, those are often rare moments—mainly because we pack our schedules so full of things that it's ridiculous.

First, there's work with all the responsibilities there. Our bosses depend on us and if we don't finish our assignments, there might be dire consequences. Not to mention stressed mornings getting ourselves and others ready for the day, and the nerve-wracking commute to and from work, with stops along the way to taxi our children to events, pick up the dry-cleaning, stop at the vet for the dog, or pick up groceries.

Once we get home, our other workload begins. Dinner

and dishes. Laundry. Homework. Cleaning. Preparing for the next day. The work never stops.

We can do it all and do it all well. Right? It doesn't matter if we've been up sick all night. It doesn't matter if a family emergency is thrown into the mix, or if a snowstorm or hurricane blows through town. We will get it all done or we'll die trying.

Are we crazy?

Why do we put such unrealistic expectations on ourselves? What even possessed us to think we could do the work of sixteen people? In a single day. With perfect results. And with our lipstick still on.

It's time for a come-to-Jesus moment. Literally. Bring your calendars, schedules, and lists, and give them all to him. Ask him to be the keeper of your schedule, to show you what he wants you to do—and not do.

You see, most of us are so busy that we're missing the important moments. Time with God. Sweet moments with those we love. Fun days with our friends. And even rest.

Thankfully, God promises sleep and rest. Yes, even to crazy people like us.

Lord, I suspect you shake your head quite often as you observe your crazy children each day. You should. Even I recognize the craziness of what I often try to accomplish. I give it all to you— my calendar, my schedule, my to-do lists, and my big dreams. I don't want to get to the end of my life and realize that I've accomplished a lot but haven't done what you wanted me to do. Give me focus. Give me an obedient spirit. Give me rest. Help me to learn the fine art of praying first to ask what you want me to do, and then saying no if it's not one of the tasks you have for me.

Are you exhausted? Do you have trouble
saying no when someone asks you to do
something? How do you think praying
about it before answering will
make a difference?

Sleep might be one of the most overlooked
aspects of health in our society. Living in a "city
that never sleeps" or pulling an all-nighter should
not be a proud badge you wear.

CHAPTER THIRTY-EIGHT

Lulled to Sleep

A young man named Eutychus, sitting at the window,
sank into a deep sleep as Paul talked still longer.

ACTS 20: 9 ESV

The church was filled with worshippers. A young father
with his family found an empty row and settled down.
Soft familiar music caressed the air. The warm building felt
snug and cozy. Soon their youngest slept, nestled into her
mother's lap. Deep contented breathing sounded from the
middle son's wide-open mouth. The father gazed at his
children, yearning to give way to the waves of sleep drawing
his eyelids down like weighted wool. Why is it that when we
least want to fall asleep we do, and when we desperately
want to, we can't?

The unwelcome grip of sleep is like torture. When sleep
doesn't happen at night, staying awake in the day becomes
almost impossible.

Being lulled to sleep at the wrong time can be downright

dangerous too, as Eutychus discovered when the Apostle Paul talked until past midnight.

Eutychus sat in the window of the upper room where a group had met together to hear Paul's message. Lamps flickered in the dim light, and the young man couldn't keep his eyes open. Overcome by sleep, he fell out the open window and dropped three stories.

Eutychus' is a much more dramatic story of falling asleep during a sermon than the young man with his family at church, but all of us can relate to both because we understand. We know what it's like to be lulled to sleep.

There is another type of being lulled to sleep that's even more dangerous. It's the kind that dulls our senses to spiritual things. God's Word nourishes our innermost being. By renewing and refreshing our spiritual lives through Scripture, we find new calm and reassurance. Reviewing Scripture is a great way to soothe minds and bring serenity to hearts.

If you find yourself barely able to keep your eyes open when they should be, yet you toss and turn unable to sleep at night, perhaps it is a spiritual wake-up call. No matter the hour of the day or night, the words of God bring rest.

Dear Father, am I lulled by things that draw me away from you? Please show me If I am. Keep me wide awake spiritually. Help me not to be lazy about what is most important. Put into my heart and mind a deep desire to read your Word and learn more about how you want me to live. Help me to put you first in my priorities. If there are ways I am not alert to your will or that I'm disobedient, convict me. Give me the awareness to change. Make me sensitive to your Holy Spirit and train me so I grow to be more like you so I learn to rest in you.

In what ways do you become lulled to sleep spiritually? How can you be more aware of your spiritual alertness?

If it takes more than twenty minutes to fall asleep experts advise getting out of bed, going to another room in the house and doing something relaxing like reading or listening to music.

CHAPTER THIRTY-NINE

Tears on My Pillow

Weeping may tarry for the night,
but joy comes with the morning.

PSALM 30:5 ESV

Still half-asleep, Rose reached over in the darkness to put her arm around her husband... and felt nothing but emptiness. She jerked awake, raw grief overwhelming her as tears soaked into her pillowcase. He wasn't there anymore. He never would be again. Rose knew Rob was with Jesus now, that he was in a better place, but that didn't lessen the pain of her sweetheart being gone.

Several months had passed since Rob's funeral. Rose still hadn't washed his pillowcase. She could nestle her head there and smell his cologne, although the scent was becoming more faint each day. He had been her whole world. How would she survive?

Perhaps you're like Rose. You've lost a sweetheart or someone close to you. Perhaps your grief is so deep that it's hard to catch your breath. You wonder if you'll ever smile again or how you'll make it through the weeks and months ahead.

But you will.

How can you know? Because many people have been where you are and they have discovered that God is faithful and his promises are true. On those lonely dark nights, God's arms will slip around you and he will dry your tears with a loving nail-scarred hand. On those days when you wonder how you'll make it by yourself, he'll say, "My child, you're not alone. I will always be with you."

Cling to Jesus, sweet friend. His love will ease the pain like nothing else can. Yes, life will be different, but the sun will shine again. You will smile, and you will laugh again. Because God will not leave you comfortless, and he will be enough for all that you're going through. As he has promised, he will give you rest—sweet rest—and joy will come in the morning. Tried and proven.

Dear Lord, I've become a member of a club I never wanted to join. Grief overwhelms me. It catches me at unexpected moments throughout the days, and the loneliness and loss overwhelm me in the night. I'm weary from the heartache, and it's even affecting my health. I miss my loved one. But you promise that you will comfort me. That you'll never leave me alone. That joy will come in the morning. I need you, Lord. I'm grateful that you're a faithful God. Comfort my aching heart. Let me feel your loving arms around me. Help me use what I learn from this time to minister to others as they go through similar experiences.

What can you do when grief overwhelms you? What promises from God's Word can you claim as your personal promises?

Studies conducted by multiple universities found that people who had recently been widowed were two to three times more likely to experience inflammation due to sleep disturbances.

CHAPTER FORTY

The Midnight Hours

When they had inflicted many blows upon them, they threw them
into prison, ordering the jailer to keep them safely. Having received
this order, he put them into the inner prison and fastened their
feet in the stocks. About midnight Paul and Silas were praying and
singing hymns to God, and the prisoners were listening to them.

ACTS 16:23-25 ESV

Paul and Silas were often treated unjustly because
of their stand for Jesus. They preached near and far,
encouraging churches and sharing the good news about
Jesus. Paul felt God leading the two of them to Macedonia to
preach to the people there. God used Paul and Silas mightily
in the town. They led a wealthy businesswoman named Lydia
to the Lord, and Paul cast out the evil spirit of a female slave
fortune-teller.

When her owners realized their money-making
opportunity was over, they seized Paul and Silas and took
them to the authorities and said, "These men are Jews, and
are throwing our city into an uproar by advocating customs

that are unlawful for us Romans to accept or practice" Acts 16:20-21, NIV.

The crowd jumped in on the action, attacking Paul and Silas, and the magistrate ordered that the two men be stripped and beaten with rods. They were flogged severely and then thrown into prison. The jailer put them in an inner cell and placed their feet in the stocks.

Imagine the scene that night. These two men—guilty only of serving God—were aching from where they'd been beaten. The inner cell was completely dark, and likely the other prisoners were yelling taunts and laughing at them.

But at midnight, in the midst of the darkness, Paul and Silas prayed, and then they did something totally unexpected. They sang. In the midst of being unjustly accused. After being beaten and locked up in an inner prison cell, they sang. And the prisoners were listening.

Can you imagine how unusual it must have been to hear people worshipping God and singing in that prison?

It's a reminder for all of us. The next time we're in our beds in the dark and we can't sleep because of difficult circumstances, we can still pray. And then we can sing praises, knowing that the God who busted Paul and Silas out of prison can bust us out of whatever situation we're in, and give us rest while he's doing it.

Lord, this story of Paul and Silas moves me to tears. After the beating they endured, their bodies must have been in severe pain as they were locked into stocks in the prison. They could have been bitter and sulked and whined (like I probably would have done), but instead, they prayed and sang. In the darkness. In that moment where there was no rest for their bodies. They sang. Father, on the nights when my spirit is wounded, or when my body is hurting, give me a song in the night, and help others hear it as I share about my faithful God. Help me to rest in you, just as Paul and Silas did so many years ago.

How can God use your physical pain or your heartache to touch the lives of others? How do you think Silas and Paul's prayers and songs affected the other prisoners?

Faith and spirituality are much more than just comforting rituals to religious individuals. They have a positive impact on mood and mental health. Aspects of faith enable tangible reductions in, and protection from, stress. Faith generates optimism, enriches interpersonal relationships, creates support systems, and enhances quality of life.

CHAPTER FORTY-ONE

On the Road Again

"I am with you and will watch over you wherever you go,
and I will bring you back to this land. I will not leave you
until I have done what I have promised you."

GENESIS 28:15 NIV

Transition is often a sleep-snatcher. Whether it be a job, stage of life, or even altered health, adjustment to life lived one way can be difficult when it changes to another. It doesn't happen overnight. It's usually a process of one foot on one side of where you have been and another on where you will be. The chasm between may not always feel like it is moving in the right direction. If you find yourself in a period of transition, you are not alone.

In Genesis 28, Jacob faced travel, trouble, and transition. After a day of travel, Jacob stretched out to sleep. He took a rock and used it for a pillow. He must have been tired. A rock for a pillow seems like a strange way to sleep. During that night God gave Jacob a special dream. In it, God promised the land where he slept, a nation, and a heritage. He gave

Jacob a glimpse of the fulfillment of his transition, while pointing toward a future Messiah.

Some personalities enjoy transition more than others. You may find change stimulating and new challenges exciting. Or you might feel a sense of loss and fear. Either response might keep you awake at night.

While one asks, "When can I start?" the other asks, "What if I fail?"

If we could see the full picture, transition might seem more appealing. On the other hand, if we could see all the happenings along our route, even the most adventurous of us would likely be uncertain.

On a rocky pillow, God gave Jacob what he needed to walk the path of transition.

God is a solid rock. We can rest our weary heads on his Word and his promises. Even as he promised Jacob, he watches over our pathway. He knows the details ahead. He knows the joys and sorrows to come. His words bring rest even in transition. "I will not leave you until I have done what I have promised you."

If you are in transition's troubled unrest, lay your head on the rock and rest tonight.

Dear Father, you know the transition I'm going through. It is tough. I feel uncertain about all sorts of things and it's affecting my rest because my mind whirls too much for me to go to sleep. I am unsure how to go forward and I can't go back. Saying good-bye to life the way it used to be makes me sad. Help me to grieve well what I'm leaving but to look ahead with joyful anticipation. I want to trust you for what I can't see yet. I am grateful you don't let me be stuck in one place, but you push me forward. Thank you for walking through this transition with me. Please give me rest in the midst of it. I know you will never leave me alone on this journey.

**How can transition affect your sleep?
How does it make a difference when you
trust Jesus with the details?**

Packing your own blanket for travel may help
you fall asleep. Like a child's security blanket,
a familiar blanket can produce a conditioned
response to sleep which may help you fall asleep
faster wherever you are.

CHAPTER FORTY-TWO

A Place of Rest

The LORD is my shepherd; I shall not want.
He makes me lie down in green pastures.
He leads me beside still waters.
He restores my soul.

PSALM 23:1–3 ESV

What is restful for you? Is there a place you like to go when you need to be refreshed? There's something special about enjoying the beauty of God's creation, and while we sit and take it in, we can almost feel the stress seeping away from us.

The Sea to Sky Highway from Vancouver to Whistler is one of those places. It's a gorgeous drive. The spectacular scenery of snow-capped mountains and breathtaking bodies of water bring a "wow" every time folks drive around another curve. God's handiwork is on stunning display along the entire highway.

It's often easy to get caught up in the big vistas that one misses the smaller—but still oh-so-special—visual treats along the way. Partway up the highway, as one heads to Squamish, there's a little pond that's slightly visible, but tucked back a bit from the road. Tyler and Amanda missed it the first time they drove up the highway, but on their second trip there, they took the time to park and trek back by the pond.

What they discovered turned out to be the most special part of their day. As they walked back to the water, they passed through a leafy canopy of autumn leaves with huge trees on either side. Because of the fall nip in the air, the picnic area was empty that day, and as they neared the pond, they realized the water didn't have a single ripple in it. Not one. It was so calm that the surface was like a mirror reflecting the yellow, green, and burgundy leaves.

Tyler and Amanda found a bench near the water and sat there, the sweet peacefulness of that day seeping into their souls. They rested. They worshipped the one who had made this beauty. And both their souls and bodies were refreshed.

Sometimes we don't have to get in our pajamas to find rest. We just need to look for Jesus. And when we find his fingerprints on the world he created, we need to make it a priority to spend time with him there, and discover rest for our souls.

Father, I thank you so much for all the beauty that you made. I'm in awe of the variety and vastness of your creation. Thank you for allowing me to enjoy it, and for the peace and rest it brings me when I spend time enjoying your handiwork. In the midst of my busy days, remind me to take time to slow down and look for you there. Thank you for the green pastures and the still waters that restore my soul. Help me to be still like those waters so I can feel your presence and rest in you.

Why is God's creation so restful? When was the last time you made it a priority to enjoy it? What can you do to make that happen more often?

Spending time in nature can help relieve stress and anxiety, improve your mood, and boost feelings of happiness and wellbeing.

CHAPTER FORTY-THREE

Peace-filled Night

In peace I will lie down and sleep,
for you alone, O LORD, will keep me safe.

PSALM 4:8 NLT

Becky was a freelance writer. She'd looked forward to a trip to the big city several states from her home, both for the work opportunity and a chance to rest a bit. She planned to interview a businessman whose products were being sold at a big convention.

The man's staff made the hotel reservations for everyone, including Becky, and she was excited when she heard what part of town they were staying in. Becky had been there many times before. It was an upscale part of the city, so everything should be really nice.

Later that week, Becky took the exit number for the luxury part of the city, but as she followed the GPS and made several turns towards the hotel address, things began to change. The shops had iron bars on their doors and windows. Paint peeled from the fronts. Awnings sagged.

Parking lots were filled with giant potholes and deteriorating asphalt. Everything looked seedy.

The hotel was only several blocks from the upscale area, but it might as well have been a world away. As Becky turned into the drive for the hotel, she noticed a questionable establishment next door, and when she walked into the hotel lobby, some of the rough-looking guests from that establishment were milling about. Becky checked in, zipped to her room, and clicked the bolt into place.

She called her husband and told him to pray. Then Becky emailed her prayer group, "I can't explain right now, but pray for my safety while I'm here!"

Becky conducted her interview and then returned to the hotel. She locked herself in her room, alone and afraid. Once she'd gotten into her pajamas, she sat on the bed and prayed, "Lord, I'm afraid. Please take care of me and help me rest." As a sweet peace swept over her, Becky settled down in blissful sleep with Jesus guarding her room.

Perhaps you're in a situation now where you're afraid. Whether it's from a health scare, finances, or abuse, Jesus promises to give you peace and rest while he watches over you.

Father, I thank you for the security of knowing that whenever I feel alone or afraid, I can trust in you. Thank you for loved ones and friends who pray for me. Help me to be as faithful to pray for them. Thank you that even in the midst of those moments where fear overwhelms me, I can know without any doubt that you will be with me. I'm so grateful for the sweet unexplainable peace that you give and for the assurance that when I lie down to rest you will give me sleep. You are such a faithful God, and I'm so blessed to know that you will always be with me.

How does anxiety and fear affect your ability to sleep? When have you experienced God's sweet peace and rest in the middle of your fears?

Anxiety can affect sleep at any time but most commonly causes difficulty in falling asleep. People with higher levels of anxiety may feel anxious all the time and have trouble staying asleep. Typically, the likelihood of waking in the night parallels your degree of anxiety.

CHAPTER FORTY-FOUR
Sick Child

The LORD sustains him on his sickbed;
in his illness you restore him to full health.

PSALM 41:3 ESV

There isn't much that disturbs a night of rest for a parent
more than having a sick child. Fevers always seem to rise at
night. Stomach bugs are notorious for arriving in the dark
hours. And sometimes there are even scarier illnesses such as
seizures or breathing issues.

Our first thought as parents is that we wish we could
be sick instead, that our precious children wouldn't have to
go through these times of illness. We want to make them
better, but we don't have the power to do that. So, we
gather our little ones on our laps. We rock them for hours,
offering what comfort we can, while our stomachs are in
knots from worry.

We tuck our children into bed with us so we'll know if
they need us, or on nights when they're extremely ill, we'll

take a pile of blankets and sleep on the floor next to them so we'll be there if they awaken or if their fevers rise.

We whisper soft words of love as we hold a little hand that feels like it's on fire. We rise every thirty minutes to give teaspoons of liquids so our children don't dehydrate. We press cool cloths on fevered brows and set alarms to wake us so we can give the next dose of medicine.

We can put our pajamas on, but it's likely there will be little or no rest for us that night. Our children are sick, and there's too much worry to rest. So, we do the one thing we can do. The most important thing. We go to Jesus in prayer.

We know where the power lies. We know who can heal. And in moments where our hearts are heavy with anxiety, when our fear is so deep it feels like we can't take a deep breath, we can place our children in God's hands, and we can rest in him, knowing that there's no safer place we could ever put them.

Lord, when my child is sick, there's no way I can rest. The worry consumes me. My heart aches as I see my child suffer. Give our doctors wisdom to know what to do. I'm so grateful that when the doctor has no answers, you are always available. Help me to trust you and to place my child in your hands. Remind me that I'm your child. That your heart aches when mine does. That what concerns me concerns you. So please touch the body of this one I love. Help the fever break. Calm the sick tummy. Ease the breathing. Touch this body you created and restore my child to full health. Provide rest for both of us.

How can having a sick child teach you to trust God more? How can Jesus provide rest in the night?

Lack of sleep can affect your immune system. Studies show that people who don't get quality sleep are more likely to get sick after being exposed to a virus, such as a common cold virus. Lack of sleep can also affect how fast you recover if you do get sick.

CHAPTER FORTY-FIVE

Attention Please

He who planted the ear, does he not hear?
He who formed the eye, does he not see?

PSALM 94:9 ESV

We live in a plugged-in society. Walk into any waiting room, and what do you see? Stand in most any line and people are doing the same thing. Try talking to a teenager in the car, or a family member sitting on the couch, and you will soon discover there is a lengthy distance from planet earth to the attention of another person. As much as technology makes up the working world, we still seek a mindless task to unwind. We plug in again.

Here comes a clearing of the throat and a drumroll. Can God have our attention, please?

Studies warn us of the effects technology has on our brains and its detriment to sleep and rest. Various new medical issues are linked to thumb movement and eye strain. Addictions are rampant. Social media drives actions and culture. But we still love our technology. In fact, most of us consider the plusses outweigh the negatives. It has our attention.

Inattention is a problem all throughout Scripture. Psalm 94 describes a contrast between followers of God and the wicked. Not only did the unbelievers not listen to God, they had the audacity to say God wasn't even paying attention anyway.

God answered their accusations. "He who planted the ear, does he not hear? He who formed the eye, does he not see?"

God is attentive. He made our ears and eyes. How ridiculous to entertain the thought that he doesn't see or hear what we do or say. He is an interactive God. He speaks to us through his Word, his Spirit and his Church. He relates to us. He wants relationship.

Time unplugged allows us to listen, relate, and think. Our brains need pauses to ponder and reflect during the day. We benefit from waiting without distraction. Complete attention requires disciplined intentionality, necessary for relationships to grow.

As you wind down for the day, set aside distractions. God hears. He sees. Give him the quiet of your mind. Let him have your nighttime attention. Stop and listen. It may be that he is asking, "Can I have your attention, please?"

Dear Father, thank you for technology. I realize having so much helpful information at my fingertips is a privilege. I have stuff coming at me constantly. I'm overloaded with everything from social media to important data. My attention goes there more often than to relationships around me, and it's even interrupting my sleep, causing me to be fatigued the next day. I have not listened to you first and foremost. Forgive me. Give me creativity in how I can pay better attention to you and others and help me to turn my technology off so I can rest and hear you speak to me in the quiet moments.

**How attached are you to technology?
In what way does it affect your rest and
the attention you give to God and others?**

95% of people use some type of computer, video
game, or cell phone at least a few nights a week
within the hour before bed. Light given off by
electronics like computers and cell phones delays
the release of melatonin and makes it more
difficult to fall asleep.

CHAPTER FORTY-SIX

Listen

I'll lie down and sleep like a baby—
then I'll awake in safety,
for you surround me with your glory.

PSALM 3:5 TPT

The baby took forever to fall asleep. The mom was amused as she walked through the room. Her husband was sound asleep, but the baby—held securely in his arms—was bright-eyed and ready to play.

On another day, the mother just shook her head as the baby camera caught her toddler in all kinds of shenanigans when he was supposed to be napping. He turned somersaults across the mattress. Looked out the window. Played with his cars. Yanked books out of the bookcase—not to read, but just to make a mess. And then, as if remembering he was supposed to be taking a nap, he climbed back onto his bed and the cycle began again.

As children become older, it's harder to get them to take a nap even though they really need it. Many a parent has had a child fall asleep at the dinner table, on the floor while playing, or even wobbling around drowsily while they're standing up.

As the teen years arrive, it's almost the opposite. It's all parents can do to drag their kids out of bed by noon, or they nap the afternoon away and then aren't ready to go to bed when nighttime comes around.

Then when they become adults and the stage of parenting hits, moms and dads would give anything to swap places and take those naps for their children. Somehow that rarely happens. But by then, we understand the importance of rest. We feel the lack of it and our bodies scream at us that we need more. With jobs, children, homes, laundry, meals, and other must-do tasks, how can we possibly find the time to rest? Shucks, we sometimes treat rest as if it's a bad four-letter word.

God promises rest to his people. He tells us to come and rest awhile—and if we don't, we truly will fall apart after a while.

Maybe it's time to listen to our heavenly Father when he says, "My child, you need a nap." Because he's probably tired of his cranky children as well.

Lord, children fight sleep, but they're young and they don't realize how much they need it. I'm an adult and I know I need it, but I fight it anyway, saying I have too much to do, that I'm the only one who can do what I do, and that I don't have time to rest. God, remind me that you designed my body to need rest. Help me to do what must be done, to delegate what others can do, and give me the wisdom to know the difference. Then help me to respect what your hands have made by getting the rest and sleep that my body requires.

Why do you make excuses for why you don't have time to rest? What happens to your body and disposition when you don't get enough rest?

If you continue to operate without enough sleep, you may see more long-term and serious health problems. Some of the most serious potential problems associated with chronic sleep deprivation are high blood pressure, diabetes, heart attack, heart failure, or stroke.

CHAPTER FORTY-SEVEN

Turn It Off

What do people get for all the toil and anxious striving
with which they labor under the sun?
All their days their work is grief and pain;
even at night their minds do not rest.
This too is meaningless.

ECCLESIASTES 2:22-23 NIV

Lynn had mentioned several times that day that she was tired, but when everyone else went to bed, she stayed up. Her son said, "Mom, you keep saying you're tired. Why don't you go to bed?" He laughed as she told him she needed some time for her mind to turn off.

Lynn had learned the hard way that if she went from the merry-go-round of her day and climbed into bed without winding down, her mind would stay busy for hours, like a kaleidoscope gone wild.

She had discovered that if she made a list of what had to be done the next day, it would clear her mind of those tasks. And she'd learned to cut her screen time before bedtime because all those cute things on Pinterest made her want to get busy making her house prettier. Heaven forbid if she got caught up in what was going on in the lives of her friends on Facebook. That could really eat up a lot of time.

Sometimes a cup of hot chocolate was just the trick to slow her mind down. She'd sit in her recliner and enjoy the stillness. Or she'd read until she was ready to go to sleep. But the best way she'd found to relax before bedtime was to pray for those she loved.

There was something special about talking with Jesus in the tranquility of those moments before bed. Praising him for who he is. For how he'd blessed her beyond what she deserved. Bringing her family's needs before him. Telling him what was heavy on her heart. Whispering those big dreams that were too personal to share with anyone else.

And then praying for family, friends, and co-workers who needed Jesus in their lives. For loved ones who were dealing with health-related issues or whose marriages were falling apart.

Do you need to turn your mind off before you go to bed? Place all your troubles in God's hands, spend some time with him, and then enjoy the sweet rest that he's promised to you.

Dear Father, thank you for always being my burden bearer. When I'm weary and discouraged, remind me to bring my concerns to you. Help me to place my loved ones in your hands, to bring you the things that are heavy on my heart. Thank you for loving me enough to spend time with me, and for always being available whenever I want to talk to you. It boggles my mind that the God of the universe loves me that much. Thank you for your strength and your faithfulness. Remind me that true rest is found in you and whenever I need to clear my mind from the craziness of my day, the best way to do that is to fill it with you.

How can a racing mind keep you from getting to sleep? How does talking to Jesus before bedtime make a difference in how you sleep?

We need to unwind in order to set the stage for sleep. Allow for at least an hour before bedtime to be protected, relaxing, wind-down time. This creates closure for the day and allows your brain to begin the process of shutting off. The process should take place somewhere outside of your bedroom with dimmed lights. Don't use anything with a screen as this can trick your brain into thinking it should still be awake. Find whatever works for you and make it a nightly routine.

CHAPTER FORTY-EIGHT

On His Throne

God reigns over the nations;
God is seated on his holy throne.

PSALM 47:8 NIV

If you want to throw something at the latest news announcement, remember Moses, Jesus, and Peter all dealt with political situations. Governing powers complicated the life of Esther, David, and Paul. Scripture is chocked full of kings, rulers, laws, and alliances which swept lands and affected God's people. Biblical history moved with the tide of evil or good, wicked or righteous, peaceful or ruthless powers. It is enough to keep us up at night.

Let's not forget, God used an evil Pharaoh to set the stage for Moses to lead the Israelites out of Egypt. A shepherd boy chosen to be the future king fled from the reigning king intent to destroy him. That boy, David, became an Old Testament ruler pre-figuring the Messiah.

Jesus was born into a political mess with a ruthless king out to kill Jesus and every other child two years and under. During Jesus' life, he was asked about the political dichotomy of paying Roman taxes. He answered by producing the money from the mouth of a fish. An alliance pacifying Roman ruler Pilate and Jewish religious authority Caiaphas set Jesus' crucifixion into motion.

Political leaders stir the pot of history past and present. Civic and world tensions toss and turn us in our beds. As much as we'd like to pull the covers over our heads and hide, politics is a part of human existence. It affects our finances, safety, and freedom. At times it looks like the whole world is in chaos, heading down a path of destruction. But the good, bad, and ugly help to remind us who is truly on the throne.

"God reigns over the nations." When the world looks grim and anxiety troubles your rest, take a moment to remember God reigns over all nations and governments.

"God is seated on his holy throne." Regardless of partisan wins or losses, God is still on his throne.

Political tweets, media broadcasts, and government bureaucracy may make us want to tear out your hair but take heart. Don't let it steal your sleep. God reigns. The throne belongs to him.

Dear Father, sometimes I get so tied up in the stuff happening in the world and politics that I forget you reign. Forgive me. The crazy situations of our government and leaders feels out of control at times. Help me to trust and believe you are in control. Thank you for being on the throne yesterday, today, and tomorrow. I know no matter what laws are in place or who puts them there, you are the sovereign ruler. Please guide our leaders to make right decisions and give me wisdom how to follow. Help me honor you and respect the people you have chosen. Thank you for reigning. Thank you for giving me sweet rest even when the world around me seems to be in chaos.

Does knowing God is on the throne change
how you feel about the world around you?
How can knowing he's in control help you
to sleep in peace despite what's happening
in the world?

Your body may give you warning signs if you are
overwhelmed by political situations or national
and world events. A higher blood pressure than
usual, weight gain or loss, anxious feelings, drastic
mood changes and sleep struggles can all be
traced to political overload.

CHAPTER FORTY-NINE

Quiet Love

The LORD your God is in your midst,
a mighty one who will save;
he will rejoice over you with gladness;
he will quiet you by his love;
he will exult over you with loud singing.

ZEPHANIAH 3:17 ESV

She longed to slide under cool sheets and forget the whole day. It had been a bust since the morning when her two-year-old had walloped her baby sister with a plastic car. She wanted to forget the angry tension transferred to her husband when he got home from work. She wished she could erase the hurtful words that spewed from her mouth. Her pounding heart and rising blood pressure longed for quiet. If only she could toss all of it into a box, label it *Bad Day*, put it away on a shelf out of sight, and go to bed.

Oh, to give into the oblivion of sleep, to forget the day and start another new and fresh. But when the children were put to bed like the toys put away for the night, her soul's disquiet rolled over her in waves.

Trouble is part of the fabric of our human existence. When we fall victim to its upheaval, it's as if trouble itself takes up residence inside us. Our souls can't find a comfortable position of rest. When we recognize we've done something wrong, disquiet grows into a loud disturbing roar.

Zephaniah, an Old Testament prophet, spoke of God's chosen people's troubled past. He exposed Judah's sin as a nation and as individuals. He prophesied judgement and unrest. But he also reminded his readers God is a God of restoration and hope. God blesses a repentant humble heart.

The picture of God's love in Zephaniah's words is calming and restorative, "He will rejoice over you with gladness; he will quiet you by his love."

The root of God's joy and ours is the sweet and intimate communion between the Father and his children. This restored relationship brings rest to our souls. God's tender love over us is a constant reality. It brings the internal peace we so desire. In effect, the bad day can be put away under the lock and key of his forgiveness.

"He will exult over you with loud singing."

Can you rest in the presence of God's loud singing over you? Most certainly.

Dear Father, I am so glad you are present with me tonight. Even when I fail, and even when I sin, you love me. I said things today I shouldn't have said. Forgive me for acting out of the disquiet of my soul rather than the quiet of your strength. Thank you for always being with me and forgiving me. Would you quiet me tonight with the indescribable love you offer? It is wonderful to know God Almighty rejoices over me. It brings me joy too. Would you sing over me tonight and bring my heart out of unrest into peace?

Have you ever imagined God singing over you? What do you think he wants his song to say to you?

Music has the power to slow your heart rate and breathing, lower your blood pressure, and it may even trigger your muscles to relax, making music the perfect preparation for restorative slumber.

CHAPTER FIFTY

Sweet Interruptions

By day the LORD directs his love,
at night his song is with me—
a prayer to the God of my life.

PSALM 42:8 NIV

Sleep is a priceless commodity. So it seems a bit crazy to tell you to look forward to interruptions in the middle of your rest, but sometimes when we can look back with the beauty of hindsight, we realize that those were some of the most priceless moments of our lives.

Have you ever had a baby at your house? Or taken care of one overnight? You'd just gotten into a deep sleep when you heard crying from down the hall. Still half asleep, you trudged to the baby's room, maybe changed a diaper, and then settled down in the rocker to feed the baby.

The soft light from the lamp highlighted the precious gift in your arms. For the first time that day, without all the other distractions, you had time to really gaze at the perfection of baby skin and rosebud lips and to stroke your hand across downy soft hair. And when the little one's tummy was satisfied, they wanted to talk with sweet cooing sounds as they gazed into your eyes. Tiny arms and legs wiggled with excitement as you talked back. What began as a weary task ended up as a delightful blessing.

Have you ever been awakened for seemingly no reason and then you can't go back to sleep? God sometimes wants to spend time with his children in the nighttime hours as well. How precious to hear his whispers, "I know things are difficult right now, but rest in me. It's going to be okay." The situation might not be better, but just knowing he's in control makes all the difference.

It's a moment to treasure when God gives you a song in the night and you quietly sing about it being well with your soul. What an indescribable gift it is when you can feel his presence hovering close, when he feels so near that you could almost reach out and touch him.

Does spending the nighttime hours with his children bring God as much joy as we have with the children around us? Likely it does.

Father, I'm tired, so I usually hate to have my sleep interrupted. But, oh my, the amazing blessings you've surprised me with in the nighttlme hours. Thank you for the priceless moments of never-to-be-forgotten times of pure sweetness. I'm so grateful for the nights when you've awakened me so that you could spend time with me. For the moments I've felt your presence wrap around me like a warm blanket. For the songs you give in the darkness. And for your overwhelming peace that all is well because you're in control. Sweet interruptions indeed.

Why do you think God sometimes awakens you in the night so he can spend time with you? What makes those nighttime hours so special?

Spending time with God at night is so important. In the quiet solitude of the darkness, he will refresh and restore you, lead you in paths of righteousness, and teach you how to enjoy every day of your life.

CHAPTER FIFTY-ONE

Unnumbered Thoughts

How precious are your thoughts about me, O God.
They cannot be numbered!
I can't even count them; they outnumber the grains of sand!
And when I wake up, you are still with me!

PSALM 139: 17-18 NLT

It's bedtime and you are ready. Your face is washed. Your teeth brushed. Those millions of thoughts spinning wildly all day make a few sluggish cycles. Tomorrow can wait. Your pin hole of consciousness closes like a camera aperture. Your muscles relax. You sink in blissful oblivion.

But waking up is a different matter. How we fall asleep doesn't guarantee how we awake. Sometimes our dawn comes long before the hour it should. Sleep won't return and night hasn't produced its hoped-for rest. Wide eyes blink into darkness. Minds take up the gerbil wheel of never-ending-new-day-ahead tasks. The stress to come brings uneasy restlessness. Weariness sets into the day before it begins.

Written for the chief musician, Psalm 139 is one of the most beloved psalms of King David. It declares an ever-present God, a perfect bedtime reminder of his sovereignty over events, a calming security to end each day, and an important morning truth. David speaks with absolute assurance. His words steady his readers, proclaiming God will never leave us.

However, perhaps nothing strikes as tender and precious as his description of a God who formed and knows us entirely. He knit us together in the dark recesses of our mother's womb. He knows when we sit, stand, and sleep. He knows each thought before it forms. David insists such absolute knowledge is too wonderful, too great, literally beyond our reach of understanding.

"How precious are your thoughts about me, O God," David wrote, amazed at the marvel of being fully known yet fully loved.

In God's constant awareness of his creation, his thoughts about us outnumber the sand. He thinks about you on your bed asleep and when you wake. If the digits on the nighttime clock read 2:00, 4:00, or 9:00, his thoughts are on you. God's presence never takes a break though dark shadows fall or bright sun shines in your eyes. His watchful care is constant and inescapable.

God's intimate surrounding wraps us like a warm embrace. His presence offers hope and comfort. Our tranquil souls find secure rest. We awake with trust.

Dear Father, thank you for your presence surrounding me. I can't fathom your thoughts for me. Thank you for knowing me completely and loving me. Your everywhere presence and all-knowing character is mind-boggling. I am so grateful you care so much for me. Thank you for knowing about where I am and what I do. Thank you for forming me with intricate love. Thank you that you are with me each night and morning. Help me live each day remembering how much you think about me. Keep how wonderful and great you are in my mind tonight and when I wake in the morning. It humbles me that I'm on your mind even when I'm asleep.

How does God show he cares for you? Describe what it means to you knowing he thinks about you. How does that make you rest with security?

Experts estimate that the mind thinks between 50,000 and 80,000 thoughts a day. That's an average of 2,100 to 3,300 thoughts per hour.

CHAPTER FIFTY-TWO

Make It Happen

Jesus told his disciples to get into their boat and to go to the other
side of the lake while he stayed behind to dismiss the people.

MATTHEW 14:22 TPT

Burdened and overwhelmed by life, we sometimes need
to make time alone happen. Intentional carved-out time
for solitude takes wisdom and determination. Jesus, on a
short life mission with the greatest purpose in the history of
humankind, took time away from his busy schedule. It didn't
just happen without deliberate action.

The busier we get, the less time we have for restorative
solitude. "Something has to give," we say, but unless we
make some difficult choices, schedules tend to control us
rather than us controlling them.

Jesus dismissed the crowds. The gospels record several
instances when Jesus, after a day of ministry separated
himself from the crowds of people surrounding him. He
needed to be alone. He connected with the Father and he
rested from constant demands. Sometimes his departure

from the larger crowds brought opportunities to speak privately with his disciples, other times it allowed him seclusion to pray or rest.

Jesus' retreats showed intentionality. He withdrew before he chose his disciples. He spent time on a mountainside by himself before he walked on water. After time alone he taught and healed. He prayed alone before soldiers came to take him away.

Jesus' busy life records times of intense ministry, when he went hungry and sleepless, but his life also shows refreshing times apart. He dismissed the crowds and found time to be alone.

In our minds, there is a paradox. In his humanity, he became weary and hungry; yet Jesus, our compassionate Savior, made it happen. He took deliberate action to tell the crowds to go home. He sought alone time. He prayed.

We live with responsibilities and demands. It is difficult to know when, what, or how to dismiss ourselves from them. We don't want to let people down and we aren't always sure how to say no. Jesus knew the boundaries in his life and can give us wisdom in understanding ours.

Perhaps this is a time when you must decide to make time for rest and re-connection with the Father. Make it a matter of intentional prayer. Find solitude and make it happen.

Dear Father, I realize I'm not really good at making time in my schedule for solitude. I am intentional about a lot of things, but I neglect some of the most important things. Help me to take time for solitude, to connect with your Spirit, read your Word, and listen to your voice. Teach me how to carve time into my days to be refreshed. Show me how to be compassionate and firm with demands from others when you want me to say no. Guide me to dismiss from my agenda what I should and add the alone time I need. Thank you for modeling prayer and rest into your busy schedule. Teach me to rest.

What could you cut from your schedule in the next few days in order to allow time for solitude? Where can you go to be alone? What can you learn from Jesus about seeking rest?

Spending time alone may actually help develop greater compassion for people. It brings you outside of your usual circle of friends and co-workers which helps you be aware of others.